for Asher

Table of Contents

FANS

Letter from the Author

P. EDWARD CLAYPOOLE

I've wanted to make movies ever since I was a little kid. To
this day, I can pretty much remember every movie I've seen in the theatre,
where I saw it and with whom. One of my favorite memories was when my
father and I were at Rehoboth Beach in Delaware and he surprised me by
taking me to see *Karate Kid* 2. Granted, not the best film ever made, but
the fact that my dad, who doesn't enjoy indoor activities, or to be honest,
movies, all that much, went out of his way to surprise me with a father-son
trip made a lasting impression on me and cemented my love for film.

During the course of my childhood there are hundreds of movies that have
shaped my life for different reasons. *The Goonies* soundtrack instantly
takes me back to childhood, playing imaginary games involving pirates
and looking for treasure. *Home Alone* has been such a huge part of my
life that I went and visited the home used in the movie on a business trip
to Chicago (wearing Macauley Caulkin's signature winter hat, of course).
Jurassic Park's unbelievable CGI still amazes me today, despite consistent
advances in the field. *Ferris Bueller's Day Off, Better off Dead, Karate Kid*
and *Stand By Me* — these are a few movies that drew me to filmmaking as
a child. As I got older and appreciated the craft more, I fell in love with *The
Color of Money, Goodfellas, Fargo, The Usual Suspects, Indiana Jones,
Seven, The Last of The Mohicans, The Shawshank Redemption* and *Beverly
Hills Cop.*

Movies are difficult to make. They include cinematography, acting, editing,
lighting, sound, music and storytelling, which all combine to create
landscapes that are viewed and interpreted by each individual differently.
All of these jobs require unique skills, and most people master only one of
them. As I child I wanted to be an actor — the super hero, detective or CIA
operative … an all-around tough guy. As I got older I found myself more
attracted to directing, cinematography and editing; anything I could do
behind the lens. If I eventually had the opportunity to write stories, then I
was finally putting my voice out there for the world to see and hear.

All of these dreams and wishes followed me to my high school graduation, at which point my path veered in a million directions. I went to school for liberal arts but eventually dropped out, not sure what I wanted to do with my life but still having that strong desire to work in film. Looking back, I think I was scared, and had already resigned myself to the fact that I would likely never make it in Hollywood. After a few years of messing around I eventually enrolled at The Art Institute of Philadelphia for video production. At that point they no longer offered a film program. There, I found a renewed ambition that I would graduate, move to Hollywood, get a job and win Oscars.

I remember a scriptwriting class in which we had to come up with a movie idea, write the first 10 pages of the script and then present it to the class. The week of the presentations my teacher called me to the front of the class and in a whisper told me: "Your idea is excellent and has the potential to be something if you can get it written and in the right hands. You do not need to present this if you don't want to. If I were you, I would keep this to myself and write it." I never did present it to the class but there I was saying to myself, "Hollywood, here I come!" It didn't work out that way.

I did really well at The Art Institute and graduated with honors in 2005. I was working part-time at a local super market and looking for jobs. I applied anywhere I could but had absolutely no luck. I was offered a few jobs with no pay — I had to get the experience before I could be paid — and I didn't take them. I always found that odd and still do, when you apply for most jobs you have to learn how the business works, but they pay you as you learn. But because jobs in film, photography and writing are considered artistic, there's this industry expectation that new graduates or anyone trying to get into the field will work for free or next to nothing to gain knowledge. It makes it unappealing in a way, but people are still willing to do it. I on the other hand had bills to pay.

I eventually found a full-time job in retail, which I hated, and I put my degree on the backburner. I figured I had the degree and it would only be a matter of time before someone called. Again, that didn't happen. I continued to look for anything I could apply for and I eventually found work filming weddings. Not exactly what I was looking for, but it paid pretty well and I was getting experience. It sucked up every Saturday during the summer for me for quite a few years, but I was able to make a really good end product. I was also able to create small movies for the bride and groom that were actually entertaining. I wasn't super excited to be doing this work, but I loved the creativity. This eventually led to some high school sports shooting and then corporate shooting.

During these shoots, I always thought about what big Hollywood directors would do in the same situation and I'd try to emulate their style in some way or another in my work. You can never go wrong with directing by Spielberg; I can't even name a movie of his that I don't like. Martin Scorsese's *Goodfellas* is a masterpiece. David Fincher, Quentin Tarantino and Christopher Nolan all have their own unique abilities which make their films, even when imperfect, interesting to watch. I am a huge fan of the editing of *Man on Fire* by Christian Wagner ... the bright over-the-top cinematography of Robert D. Yeoman, a frequent collaborator of Wes Anderson and of M. Night Shyamalan's creative storytelling. These are just a few of the people I really admire and always look forward to their work.

While I was working in retail and doing videography on the side, I was still unfulfilled. I wanted to create something that was my own. This is why I went to school in the first place. This was my dream as a child; it remains my dream now. I have a lot of different ideas, but the story I eventually chose to tell was a somewhat personal one, one that could have caused conflict within my family if it wasn't done properly. It took some hard decisions to continue with the project but with the help of my cousin, Rip Saling, we moved forward together.

Going into this project we both had our own unique skills we could bring to the table. What I quickly learned was we had to be experts at everything, we didn't have a budget for a cinematographer, editor or lighting engineer, that was all on us. Even though movies have gotten a lot less expensive to make since the digital age, you still have to learn all of the other skills to be able to complete a project. When I was at school I got an overview of everything — a little lighting, a little editing, a little directing. It was up to me to continue to develop those skills over time, which I continue to work on today. I have some great skills, average skills and poor skills, but overall I'm still able to make them all work and continue to make projects I'm proud of. Because of this I want to continue to be in the film industry and create projects I'm passionate about.

I learned quite a few new things during this project and I want to share those with you later on in the book, but I also wanted to talk to other filmmakers and find out their learning process. What were their highs and lows. This book will speak with independent filmmakers on one project they did. Hopefully, if you are considering making something of your own, this book will give you insight and help guide you through it. ◆

Filmmaking

PART 1

Jennifer Barbaro

THE PERFECT MATCH (2013) | DOCUMENTARY

Synopsis: Following his calling from God, Patrick McFarlane finds himself homeless, living out of the back of his truck with two wiener dogs. In complete desperation, he places an ad on Craigslist, after his seven-year journey to donate a kidney remains unfulfilled.

Was there a specific time in your life when you realized that you wanted to be a filmmaker?

Yes, actually my background started with still photography. I've been taking photographs for as long as I can remember. I was probably around six when my mom handed me my first point-and-shoot camera and I just fell in love with it, I couldn't shoot enough. I did not know at that point that this would lead to a career in film. Around age 11 I realized that I wanted to be in front of the camera and I wound up doing a lot of auditions and theatre, and by 14 I had done a lot of Philly commercials and basically any acting gigs I could find around the Philadelphia area. After completing my first two years of college, I knew I wanted to be in the film industry and needed to move to Los Angeles.

Did you go to school for film or video production, and was it what you expected it to be?

After being accepted to a few universities around the Philadelphia area, I decided last-minute to apply to schools in LA, where I completed my undergrad degree. My BA actually combined my interest in fashion/wardrobe with many classes in film, writing and communications. During college and for a few years after, I continued to work both in front of, and behind, the camera. I got a few agents and earned my SAG/AFTRA membership. I was able to pay my bills, doing what I loved. It was a way to be on set and learn things. It was also a great way to meet people who were involved in the film business such as agents, directors, producers and production assistants. During this time I networked with everyone and anyone, taking any film-related job I could get, while absorbing industry knowledge from as many perspectives as possible.

I ultimately applied to graduate schools specifically in film, and earned my master's in communications and film production from Loyola Marymount University. Going into it, I wasn't sure what to expect, but for me personally it was one of the best things I have ever chosen to do. What I really loved about Loyola's program is that each student in the graduate program was required to make a film each year, and it was a three-year program. So that meant that each person wrote, produced and directed their own film each year, based on parameters the school gave, but you owned it. Many schools I applied to offered a co-op type system, where by some process of selection one person becomes the director and the other people are assigned different roles on the film. In many of those cases, the school actually owns the film rights. Loyola's program allowed me to further learn how to manage and work each position. Film school allowed me to ask many questions in an industry that can be intimidating and sometimes does not allow room for a lack of knowledge or mistakes. This, to me, is an advantage to school in likely any field … the room to grow and become confident in a somewhat safe environment. However, I'm not sure that for me just school, or just work experience, would have made me the filmmaker and person I am today. Each experience combined contributed to my success and was an important part of the process.

What attracted you to the topic of *The Perfect Match*?

I have learned through school and real life that its easiest to write about something you know, something that is close to you or has affected you. While I did not know anything about the medical field, kidney loss or kidney function, what I did know was that my husband's mother was down to five percent kidney function and she desperately needed a kidney. Because of her age, the waiting list and the way the medical system is set up, it is very difficult to get an organ at the exact time you need one in order to save your life. So this story started because I had been personally watching my mother-in-law deteriorating and desperately in need of a kidney.

Before you shot a single scene, what were the first things you did to get up and running?

The very first thing I did was speak to the people involved to find out if they would be interested in participating. In this particular instance, had they not all been interested in participating, I may or may not have told the story because it was personal.

Did you have a budget? Did you do any fundraising?

Going into this documentary I did not have a budget. Until the kidney donor came to fruition, I didn't see a story. I wasn't looking for a story, I was just worried about my mother-in-law, and it really didn't become a story until the potential donor came into the picture. Once he was a real possibility, everything sped up, and I realized if I wanted to turn this story into a film, I needed to do it immediately. So there wasn't much time to figure out a budget or determine what a budget would be. This is not the way I normally work, but when an opportunity arises, as a filmmaker I would rather pursue the opportunity than let it go. However, as soon as I realized that I was going to make this film, I assembled a list of my anticipated needs in terms of equipment, travel and stock, put together a rough budget and set aside a certain amount of money that I considered reasonable, based on my past experience, to do the film. Once you have produced some substantial projects and know the relationships you have in the industry to barter and make requests, understand places where you may need to pad a bit and know your capacity for the minimal crew and equipment you need on average to get the job done, it is fairly easy to quickly and efficiently project your necessary budget. It just comes with experience.

What was the biggest unforeseen problem?

The biggest problem was that everything happened so fast and the story itself progressed literally overnight. It went from the idea that Mom might get a kidney in six months to a year, to the fact that she was getting a kidney in four or five days. There was literally no time, so a lot of the filmmaking had to be done in a short amount of time.

How long did the project take you and was it longer or shorter than you expected?

It took about one year to complete, which was way longer than what I expected because I didn't get to plan out the script ahead of time. Even though the story may change during the process or during post, I generally like having an outline so that I am clear on the story I am telling and the overall message I want to convey. There were some days that I was trying to do everything myself like lighting and sound. This complicated things a bit in post because while I am familiar with audio, it is not my specialty. This caused some issues that I needed to work around and delayed the completion of the film.

How many film festivals did you submit to and how many did you get into?

I believe I submitted to four and got into three. I won Best Feature Documentary for First Glance Film Festival and another festival gave me an Honorable Mention.

What did you learn from the film festival process?

I think one of the things I learned is that film festivals are looking for specific criteria. You can have the most fantastic film out there but it doesn't mean its going to get into every film festival. One of the things that is really important is to review each festival, look at their previous films, look at their film categories and read their mission statement. Does your film fit into one of their categories? Entering festivals can be costly and time consuming. When you enter and are accepted to festivals appropriate to your film and filmmaker goals, festivals can be a wonderful way to get your work out there as well as network with other industry professionals.

What was your most memorable or enjoyable moment during this process?

My favorite moment was when I was able to film the morning of my mother-in-law getting her kidney. It was very raw and very real. She was scared. The donor was scared. It was very emotional. For me, even if this wasn't my mother-in-law, it still would have been extremely emotional. As a filmmaker it was really exciting but extremely difficult both tactically and mentally. I was filming in the hospital, in surgical areas, where things needed to be sterile and privacy laws were in place. There's definitely still an excitement to guerilla filmmaking.

What advice would you give a new filmmaker getting ready to tackle their first project?

One of the most important things is organization and communication. For me, I'm a bit old-fashioned, but I have a paper binder that is my bible. Every single thing that I'm going to do from production to direction is in that bible. So every release form, every idea, every script and every update is in that. To me, the more organized you are, the more that you can be a leader on your own film and get your point across. ◆

Brock Grossl

Synopsis: This film is the story of a maniac who has escaped a mental hospital and goes on a killing spree with his hammer.

Was there a specific time in your life when you realized that you wanted to be a filmmaker?

It began when I got an old hand-me-down video camera from my grandma and I started playing around with that. When I saw *Dawn of the Dead* for the first time in high school, it opened up my love affair with horror movies but also for underground movies in general that I didn't know were out there. That was the point where I knew it was something I wanted to do and that was the path I wanted to go down.

Did you go to school for film or video production, and was it what you expected it to be?

I went to the University of Utah film program. I learned a lot, and being able to have access to supplies and equipment and other people to help and get experience was great. I think I would have been better off if I had just pursued getting work in the industry in some way instead of doing four years of the film program, but it's different for everyone. I wouldn't discourage people from going, but at the same time I think you can learn just as much if not more getting out there and doing it. With YouTube these days, there are so many people out there sharing their tricks and experiences.

What attracted you to the topic of *Brainsick, The Hammer Killer*?

It was kind of just an idea I had. I was into all those crazy old slashers and Italian Giallo movies. The look of them is great and just the fun of trying to find ways to brutally kill people. I'm not a violent person in life at all, but there is something about those special effects and as you've seen with *Brainsick*, it's something I dove into headfirst trying to do. I worked on it with a friend of mine, Devin Hummel, who wrote the short. We were going to try to make a fake trailer and then a feature but by the time the short was done we were burned out and nothing else came of it.

Before you shot a single scene, what were the first things you did to get up and running?

Getting the short down on paper, getting that blueprint to work with. Then chipping away at it from there, trying to find the people, trying to find a little bit of money to pay actors with. It took a long time to get those effects ready, trying to get permits … the Lovers' Lane scene in the movie was a nightmare; we had to run generators for hours so getting permits was a pain and a big learning experience.

Did you have a budget? Did you do any fundraising?

This was all Devin Hummel and my own pocket money. I took a full-time job just to earn the money to pay for this. We didn't try to do a fundraising campaign. I tried keeping track of the books but it got out of hand quickly. I would say we each spent about $800–$1,000. Those special effects are really expensive and that drained a lot. The little things can start adding up, too … rentals, props, gas, materials, corn syrup, food coloring, etc. It's just a handful of money here and there, but it really can sneak up on you at the end of the day. Because to see that price tag on such a crappy short film might seem excessive, but I really feel like we skimped as much as we possibly could throughout the whole process.

What was the biggest unforeseen problem?

The lack of crew and help. The girl in the car in Lovers' Lane was 17, so we ran into issues with running late at night filming. The time it took, and long shoots, people getting tired and frustrated.

How long did the project take you and was it longer or shorter than you expected?

I would say about eight months total for the whole project. It was a lot longer than we expected. We added some scenes in the beginning that we felt made it complete in a way. We didn't even have an idea for the music at first until we had a rough cut, and then we got out a keyboard and started making that John Carpenter synth stuff, which wound up taking some time.

How many film festivals did you submit to and how many did you get into?

I would guess about 15–20 and it got into maybe 5–7 different film festivals.

What did you learn from the film festival process?

I think the one fortunate thing was ours was a niche genre film. Get in on those early deadlines because its less expensive. You have to pick the ones that will work for you and hopefully they will.

What was your most memorable or enjoyable moment during this whole process?

I think getting the shot where the security guard gets his head bashed and the camera tracks to the radio, and then the face rips, just how I envisioned it. Those are the highlights, working really hard on those effects, and having them pay off.

What advice would you give a new filmmaker getting ready to tackle their first project?

Don't be afraid to put yourself out there and ask people for favors. Be willing (within reason) to impose if you need something — a prop or gear. Be willing to suck it up and ask for help, because you're going to need help from every corner, especially if you're working with no budget. They may not be willing to give it to you, but at least you tried. Be resourceful, you don't need the best lights and equipment; if you're clever and creative and have some talent you can get around that. ◆

Amy Frear

ANOTHER TIME (2015) | COMEDY

Synopsis: A twenty-something woman who may or may not be a lost time traveler deals with commitment issues and indecision in present day Philadelphia.

Was there a specific time in your life when you realized that you wanted to be a filmmaker?

I remember very clearly as a 10-year-old knowing that I wanted to be involved in film on the acting side of it. I grew up in a place where there wasn't a lot of live theatre, but once I started to go see plays when I was a teenager, I knew that acting was what I really wanted to do. I studied acting for a very long time, and then I started working on independent films when I was living in Seattle. I just loved being on the film set so much and eventually that led me to starting to write in the hopes that I could get something made. Eventually a friend suggested that I should try directing something I wrote myself, and that's pretty much what happened with *Another Time*.

Did you go to school for film or video production, and was it what you expected it to be?

I got my undergraduate degree in theatre and I have my MFA in acting, so I did not go for filmmaking. I really enjoyed being able to study theatre and acting in my days at university and I teach acting and acting for camera at the university level now, too. I will say that when I was in graduate school I had a professor who when we were studying film acting, he would have all of us be our own film crew, so two people would do a scene that day and the rest of the class would have to fill out the crews, so we would have to hold the boom or script supervise or AD and that was my first introduction to film set work and I was very grateful for that.

What attracted you to the topic of *Another Time*?

This was a time in my life when I had just moved very half-heartedly back from the west coast to the east coast; I wasn't even sure it was going to be a permanent move but financially it became a permanent move when I couldn't find my way back. I started to do some regional theatre so I had gigs in different places all the time. I think there was one year that I had 11 different addresses in six different states. I was just really all over the place, staying on lots of friends' couches and just not sure where I wanted to end up. I ultimately came to the realization that I was just going to have to make a decision in order for my life to begin, that just committing to a place and a time would start to put other things in motion and the more I wavered the more things weren't going to happen. That had a lot to do with the themes. The main character thinks she's a lost time traveler so she's trying to find her way back and super non-committal to anything that's happening in her life, so I knew that was the story I wanted to tell. When I was in college I worked as a historical tour guide in Philadelphia, and I still occasionally pick up gigs doing that now and then when I need some extra money. I knew all of the historic spots and the reenactors that work there and run them so I decided to set the film there. It made it pretty easy to film in those historic locations.

Before you shot a single scene, what were the first things you did to get up and running?

The first thing I did was a Kickstarter to start getting funds. I started putting a team together — cast, crew, securing locations — but I definitely jumped right into storyboarding as well. Because I was acting in the film as well, I wanted to make sure I was overly prepared in terms of what I wanted each shot to look like since I wouldn't really be able to be behind the camera. The DP was a good friend of mine and we also rehearsed every scene just the two of us; we would walk through the choreography — what the camera is doing and what the actors are doing. That was extremely helpful and I do think we were really prepared. I also rehearsed with my actors. I wasn't able to rehearse with my actors at location, but I would meet with them at coffee shops and go over the script and the characters' intentions and actions and also why the film meant a lot to me so that I could get them excited about it as well.

Did you have a budget? Did you do any fundraising?

I had a budget that I perhaps saw myself going over, but I knew how much money I wanted to ask for and how much I thought I would be able to get. My goal was $5,000 on Kickstarter and I ended up raising more than $6,000. I was very lucky in that people in Philadelphia were really excited about a movie being made about Ben Franklin and time travel and also having to do with a 20-something young woman dealing with commitment issues and connecting all of that. We were lucky enough to get the local media to feature our Kickstarter campaign, including *philly.com*, *Philadelphia Magazine* and the now defunct *City Paper*. They were all really excited about it, and the fact that I was a tour guide as well. I didn't quite plan on that when I was filming the Kickstarter but it really did work out that I had this sort of niche that got people excited and helped me reach my goal fairly quickly.

What was the biggest unforeseen problem?

We had a card that just malfunctioned, and we lost access to half a day of shooting on our final day, so footage was just lost. I don't know what we could have done differently except maybe have someone that's backing up footage right away. It was our final day of shooting. We had no more money, one of the actors was from New York, we were renting all of this equipment … a reshoot seemed really hard or we were going to have to spend a lot of money we didn't have. The day after we were done shooting, I got an email from someone who had been contacting me during my Kickstarter campaign saying he wanted to donate money to the film but then he just kind of fell off the radar for a while. He emailed me the next day after we had lost all of this footage and was just like, "Hey are you still making that movie? I'd like to donate some money now." It turns out he was donating a lot and we were able to use all of his money to pay for the reshoot. That was a scary day when we thought everything was lost and I think it just happens sometimes working digitally; you lose things and it's out of your control.

How long did the project take you and was it longer or shorter than you expected?

I wrote the script in June or July of 2013 and I didn't show it to anybody for a few months. We did the Kickstarter in January 2014, made it in April and I finished everything in October 2014, so about a year and five months. It was about how long I had planned.

How many film festivals did you submit to and how many did you get into?

I had six festivals it was selected for and 16 that it was not, so that's 22 festivals I applied to on Film Freeway. When I was using Withoutabox there was a few more on that.

What did you learn from the film festival process?

I really think that this film is a good film to show in front of an audience. I don't think it's the kind of short film that is going to do well online. Things don't really start cooking until 5 minutes into the film, and then I can feel the audience liven up; I can hear laughter and I think that how much I cared about this film really comes across to people. I didn't get too much negative feedback during live screenings, but definitely people that watched it for screeners told me it was too long. I really enjoyed being able to screen this film; I thought it was a lot of fun sitting in the theatre and listening to people react.

What was your most memorable or enjoyable moment during this process?

I met some really sweet people from doing this and people that said it meant something to them. It was really fun at the Trenton Film Festival because they screened my second film and this film in the same program. The DP who shot both of my films came with me, and it was really neat to see the films up against each other and to just hear people compare the two films, drawing comparisons and themes between them that I had never really thought about. That was super fun and interesting.

What advice would you give a new filmmaker getting ready to tackle their first project?

I would suggest making a film about something you really really care about. Not just making a film just because you want to make a film. Making a film about a topic or subject that means a lot to you, and that you can get other people excited about as well. I also recommend finding a group of people that you really want to work with. I recommend taking advantage of all you have at your disposal in your day-to-day life … start thinking about interesting locations and characters in your own life that you can really take advantage of on film. I would over prepare, prepare for anything and just be able to roll with the punches when things start going awry. ◆

Catalina Jordan Alvarez

PACO (2016) | COMEDY

Synopsis: This film is the story of Paco, who is a catcaller, and has a fetish of people bouncing on his lap.

Was there a specific time in your life when you realized that you wanted to be a filmmaker?

As a child I wanted to be an actress and singer. I made home movies, dance films and fashion shows, and sometimes I played a host or DJ, but I did not have the concept of being a film director as a child.

Did you go to school for film or video production, and was it what you expected it to be?

For my undergraduate degree, I studied theatre at NYU and I found out that I really enjoyed experimental theatre. After graduating from college I moved to Berlin, Germany, where I met some documentary filmmakers, and I thought that sounded like something I wanted to try. In the beginning I attempted to teach myself Final Cut Pro, but I was totally lost. I heard from a friend of mine about a self-organized unofficial film school where people would teach each other or had a teacher/professor come and teach a film skill. In 2006, it cost 50 euro a month, which was not much more than $50.00 USD. At that point, I had moved back to the States but I applied to the film school. They had five tracks corresponding to the major goals in the film school, and I was going to apply to editing and cinematography, but the same friend who introduced me to the school, convinced me to apply to the directing track. I had been doing performances in Berlin and she thought they were very creative and that I had good ideas and would make a good director. That's where I wound up studying for three years. Later I went back to the States and I applied to grad school. I did an MFA in media arts at Temple University in Philadelphia.

What attracted you to the topic of *Paco*?

Paco wound up being my first semester film at Temple. I decided that I should write a film for my brother, who's an actor. My brother is very funny and this script in a way was something I was very comfortable writing; it was very natural. It was inspired by an inside joke with my brother about a thing we used to do when we were younger. We would imitate men on the street that were beckoning people, they would say "Linda," which means beautiful in Spanish. When my brother and I were little, it more referred to a man calling a woman, or a young girl, beautiful, and we would take turns saying it to one another. Then unlike in reality where you just ignore them, or just sort of smile, we would approach the catcaller and live out some strange story where we embrace or hug them.

Before you shot a single scene, what were the first things you did to get up and running?

I had to cast it. The casting was part of the development of the script. All of the characters were originally young women besides Paco. I got bored of that and at some point I was willing to cast someone regardless of their gender, because I was interested in playing with the identities of those who would interact with Paco. I had a next-door neighbor who was very interesting and thought she would be very good at being an actor. She wound up being a wonderful actress when she read the script. So, I cast my neighbor and her nephew who played the little boy, and his real father played his dad, and I also cast my partner to get catcalled by Paco. None of them were professional actors except for my brother. I had to then figure out locations which included the playgrounds. I had to figure out the crew. I had a classmate who I liked to work with who wound up being the cinematographer. The two of us worked on the storyboard together. I also had to get an assistant camera and sound recordist, and one assistant director. Everyone except for the sound recordist was in my graduate class. One of my housemates did the shopping and cooking; she made breakfast and lunch. I also had to learn how the camera worked, I hadn't used this particular one before. We also had to figure out what type of film we wanted and how many rolls we needed. Last was costumes. There was a lot of work before we shot a single scene.

Did you have a budget? Did you do any fundraising?

I did not raise any money. I had to pay out of pocket for my brother to fly in from Los Angeles, as well as for the food and cook. Everyone else worked for free because we were in the class together. The only other expenses were in post-production. I used a grant for color correction and the Digital Cinema Package. There were also the costs for sending them to film festivals, but I got distribution grants from Temple University since this was my first semester film.

What was the biggest unforeseen problem?

One of the biggest issues was how cold it was outside. There were no bathrooms for the crew. One day we had forgotten to get a light meter from the equipment office so we had to download an app and expose the film according to what the app said which may or may not have been that accurate. In the end we did have some film that was over and underexposed that we did our best to fix in the color correction. Usually there are more headaches but our shoot went pretty smoothly.

How long did the project take you and was it longer or shorter than you expected?

I might have started writing it in October 2014 and it premiered in March 2016. For my class at Temple, I was able to put together a really rough cut; when my class was over I still didn't even have all of the original film back. Later, once I got all of the film back, I began syncing audio and cutting it together more. In the summer of 2015 I started showing rough cuts to friends in Berlin. The sound design and color correction took place in early 2016 and then it premiered at the Philly Film Showcase which was in March 2016.

How many film festivals did you submit to and how many did you get into?

I entered more than 100 festivals and it got into 30. A lot of the festivals it screened at came after it had gotten into one significant festival. When it was accepted into Fantastic Fest and Slamdance, I received a lot of emails asking me to submit to their film festivals for free, so then I didn't have to pay for it.

What did you learn from the film festival process?

I found attending film festivals very fun. There are certain festivals that have more perks than others. I learned at Temple that you have to submit to as many festivals as possible, not just a couple.

What was your most memorable or enjoyable moment during this whole process?

What I enjoyed most were the interactions with the people who helped me make it. I got to know my neighbor, I got to see my brother and I got to work with my partner. I love the collaborative nature of film and the interactions with other artists one has when making films. It's also wonderful being recognized at festivals, it makes the whole process rewarding.

What advice would you give a new filmmaker getting ready to tackle their first project?

My advice is to not imitate other films, don't try to make a film the right way — experiment. Don't follow a formula, try to make something you've never seen before. ◆

Josh Smith

FOUR THORNS FOR AIDAN (2007) | DRAMA

Synopsis: This film is the story of Aidan, who is dealing with emotions over the loss of his family. One day he steals a car, and unbeknownst to him there is a young girl in the back. The story follows how their relationship forms and the consequences he must face for making this decision.

Was there a specific time in your life when you realized that you wanted to be a filmmaker?

When I was young I wanted to be an architect. I didn't know my interests were in the creative arts until my senior year of high school. It was then that I found an interest in film production as a medium to tell a narrative that could incorporate other mediums like photography and web design. When it felt to me that filmmaking was the intersection of multiple mediums, it piqued my interest.

Did you go to school for film or video production, and was it what you expected it to be?

I graduated from Drexel University with a bachelor's of science in film production. It met or exceeded my expectations. I wasn't looking for a school that focused exclusively on theory, rather I was looking for a school that taught how to use the technology at hand to support the narrative.

What attracted you to the topic of *Four Thorns for Aidan*?

I wanted to explore the impact that decisions have on relationships, as well as the nuances of nonverbal interaction.

Before you shot a single scene, what were the first things you did to get up and running?

I filmed this in my last year at Drexel. I graduated early, so I had an entire semester to focus on just this project. It was very much 90% preparation and 10% execution. The majority of work was done prior to filming, which included building the right team, location scouting, auditioning, rehearsals, script refinement, procurement of props and costumes, etc.

Did you have a budget? Did you do any fundraising?

I had $5,000 of my own money.

What was the biggest unforeseen problem?

You have to think on the fly when you are making a film. If you are a director, one of your requirements is to prepare for known risks and have contingencies for unknown risks, so when something goes south, you can guide the team through it. The size any issue becomes is a direct reflection of the director's ability to manage the situation and the accompanying emotions.

One night, we were shooting on the Main Line and then heading into Philadelphia to shoot. The car with most of our production equipment broke down on the highway. I was sitting there with the production crew on the side of the road while my cinematographer had the camera and actors at the location in Philly. That was the biggest complication during our filming. It was then that I had to trust that I had employed the right people for the right job, and that they were prepared to carry on in my absence. So I wasn't there when that scene was shot. But we had prepared in advance what the scene would look like so they could handle it without me, and they did it well.

How long did the project take you and was it longer or shorter than you expected?

From conception to filming was about three months. Filming took a week, editing took about two weeks. After that, a friend reached out to score the film for us, so that took some additional time. Overall, it met my expectations — those lengths were what we had planned for, though I can't say there weren't some sleepless nights to pull it off.

How many film festivals did you submit to and how many did you get into?

I had factored film festivals into the budget. I entered probably 30-40 and made it into eight. I attended every one that I could. In the ideal state I would have attended all of them. The festival I really regret not attending was the West Chester Film Festival. At the time I was employed by a production company in Tokyo to write screenplays, so I wasn't even in the country when that festival was held. My advice to my past self would've been to truly commit to being at any festival you apply to in the event you are selected.

What did you learn from the film festival process?

Your opportunities are expanded through the connections you make at those events, and you need to prepare yourself for those advantages by being professional. The first interpersonal skill most students are confronted with out of college is general professionalism. Whether it's cordial and responsive communication, or being on time to events and meetings, or dressing for the occasion, when you have the opportunity to attend an event where a body of people have decided to celebrate your work, it's incredibly important, if not a social duty, to reciprocate that honor. And when you do, it pays off in the relationships that follow.

What was your most memorable or enjoyable moment during this whole process?

It was sitting down one evening after a long day and having a good meal with the cast and crew. We were all together and just elated at the day, exhausted but enjoying each other's company. To witness your own part in creating those connections that will last beyond your film — those relationships — that was as much of a success if not more than the film itself.

What advice would you give a new filmmaker getting ready to tackle their first project?

As a director, when you're writing a screenplay and auditioning and getting your team together, you need to continually challenge the moments you want on the screen and the underlying subtext of those moments, because they are not the same thing. People don't clearly reveal themselves in real life, and how we behave doesn't always match what we intend. As filmmakers, when we start writing stories, we can effortlessly make the intent the behavior, and the script ends up being exposition. Our characters end up communicating exactly what they are thinking and how they feel to each other and that's just not what happens in real life. Most of the time we don't say anything, we just express it with our behavior. As a screenwriter you need to think about those interactions and the myriad of behaviors that can lead to the same meaning and intent. And when you rehearse with your actors, you need to help them work through that intent, and seek their feedback from their perspective. They will often have better ideas, because all of us are smarter than any one of us. ◆

Carrie Brennan

BLOCK (2020) | DRAMA

Synopsis: After coming to terms with the fact that she's gay one night at school, Kit O'Brien's closeted-ness becomes personified in the form of a 30-pound cement cinder block. Invisible to everyone else but her, Kit realizes that the only way to shake this burden is to face her fears — by coming out. What starts off as a fight to show her true colors to the world, turns into a remarkable journey of release, acceptance and celebration.

Was there a specific time in your life when you realized that you wanted to be a filmmaker?

Yes. I was in seventh grade and it was the time that I started realizing I might be gay. So besides all of the normal hormonal changes that every seventh grader has, I had this other huge thing I was dealing with. I specifically remember one night while I was watching *Grey's Anatomy* with my mom, that there were these two characters who were introduced on the show — two really good looking and successful surgeons — who just so happen to be gay. Seeing these two women surgeons on this show at this time, when even just the thought of possibly being gay was the scariest thing in my life, provided me with a small ray of light. The fact that there was a message that was coming directly to me, without me outwardly looking for it, was a life-changing moment. I realized, "That's what I want to do. I want more stories out there in the world that will reach people like me." I want to tell stories that instill hope in people that can inspire people to see the best in themselves.

Did you go to school for film or video production, and was it what you expected it to be?

I studied public relations in college. While in college I got in as many student films as I could, but I did not have any type of formal training. After college I did a two-year acting program at Playhouse West Philadelphia.

What attracted you to the topic of *Block*?

I chose this specific story because I felt like there was a need for a coming out love story that grew outside the normal narrative between two people. In other words, all of the queer coming out stories I grew up watching always involved someone overcoming their fear of coming out of the closet, because their love for another character was greater than their fear of whatever would happen to them. When I was younger and was having thoughts that I might be gay, I always thought I was going to wait for that person to come around, and then I'd come out with them and it would be easier. But that person never came around. I was in the closet for 10 years, which is a long time, so I wanted to tell a story specifically about one person's inward struggle of coming to terms with themselves — the reality of the struggle, but also the liberation one feels when they do something for themselves and because they accept themselves.

Before you shot a single scene, what were the first things you did to get up and running?

While I was growing up and going through these changes in my life, I had journaled everything. Then for a while I tried to nail down what the premise of the story would be. Basically asking myself, why do I need to tell this story and what is the central message that I'm going to give people? I took all of this and worked on my timeline which took about a year. From this outline, I was able to write the script. Once I had the script finalized I went into the pre-production process.

Did you have a budget? Did you do any fundraising?

We did have an overall budget which was $10,000. We used Indiegogo which is a great site. We wound up with $15,000. After the campaign we had other events and donations after the fact, so in total our budget rounded out to about 20K.

What was the biggest unforeseen problem?

The biggest unforeseen problem I think was pulling together the moving parts for the scenes and locations. We had nine different locations, and three separate party scenes. Two of our days had gotten rained out, so our rain schedule was very tight. I would always say if you can, leave an extra day for pickup shots just in case.

How long did the project take you and was it longer or shorter than you expected?

We only had six days to film because that's how long we had the camera. I had a lot of reservations on whether or not we could get it done in this time frame but our team was incredible. So diligent, no egos, everyone just committed to telling this story and the integrity of the production. I would say as a side note on a more overall general level, no matter what phase of the process you're in, focus on what you can give, versus what you can get. People were so much more willing to help us along the way — whether it be donating a space, or giving us an extremely nice camera for the fraction of the price, or offering their time and talents on set because we didn't just want to "get our movie made." We want to give people a story that inspires them. That hopefully resonates with them, and makes them feel more alive. More connected. More okay with themselves, and being on their own journey. So overall, just focusing on what you can give the world will naturally allow things, people and places to open up to you.

How many film festivals did you submit to and how many did you get into?

We got into 13 festivals and we applied to around 50.

What did you learn from the film festival process?

I learned that the festival circuit doesn't have to be the "end all be all" of your movie. I've seen so many people pour their blood, sweat and tears into a story, put it on the festival circuit and then after two years it goes into the "indie film graveyard," where it sits in a Google drive link never to be watched again. There is so much more to the lifespan of a story than just the festival circuit. Since we made the film, I've screened *Block* at universities, middle schools, parent associations, faculty groups, queer communities in Brooklyn, big corporations and small companies, the backyards of random bars — and each time the experience felt fulfilling.

A story is a story, regardless of how many laurels you get to put on your poster. It lives and stays alive as long as you want it to. And that's the beauty of film.

What was your most memorable or enjoyable moment during this process?

The last night we were at Fenn's Coffee (in West Chester, PA). We did the last scene and when we wrapped it was like the greatest feeling I've ever had, because I was surrounded by all of these people that I love and care for so much. The AD was the second person I have ever come out to. I had gone to a film festival three years ago at Sprout Music Collective and I saw her film. This was when I was first thinking of my story. So I asked her to get coffee, because I figured here is this artist who lives here close to me; if I tell her my idea she'll get it. I sat with her on a bench at Fenn's Coffee, and I told her I was gay and that I wanted to write a movie about it. Fast forward three years later and here we are, wrapping up my film at Fenn's Coffee. She took me outside to that bench and asked me if I had remembered that conversation from three years earlier, and I had completely forgotten about it. We both burst into tears and it was just an amazing feeling.

What advice would you give a new filmmaker getting ready to tackle their first project?

Find out what you have to say and focus on what you can give people. If you don't know why you are telling your story, it's not going to resonate with people. Every month I would write down my goals, and why I had to tell my story. That goal has turned into the main plotline of my story. That plotline runs so deep that everyone on my team knows why we are telling this story. Instead of pushing our story on people, pushing our trailer on people and then asking for money, we said how can our story add value to your life? How is it going to change your life? So for filmmakers, I think instead of focusing on what you can get from people, focus on what you will offer people. ◆

Lynn Blackwell Denton

SCUMBLING (2006) | DRAMA

Synopsis: This film is the story of Anne, an aspiring artist, who returns home after spending time in a psychiatric hospital. As she tries to begin her healing process with her family, she continues to battle demons, while seeking her artistic dreams.

Was there a specific time in your life when you realized that you wanted to be a filmmaker?

No. I didn't know what I wanted to do except I was into a lot of creative areas. I enjoyed painting and that was one of my first loves. I also enjoyed performance, plays and skits, and directing skits in school and orchestrating a whole thing with music and dialog and actors; I did a lot of that in high school. I didn't know what I would end up doing. When I first started out, a possibility was dress design. I made all of my own clothes and I loved fashion and fabric. But I loved so many different things and film really brings those things together. I didn't find that out until much later in my life. When I got my MFA at the University of Tennessee in painting, there was no film department, but I was thinking about it then because I spent a lot of free time going to TV stations and getting their old reels of commercials and cutting them together to make a collaged film. That was totally outside of everything else that I was doing, but I was just interested and curious about that.

Did you go to school for film or video production, and was it what you expected it to be?

When I was in graduate school I did not, but 25 years later, I had this desire to go back and learn about film, so I enrolled at Temple University and took courses there. I took the courses I felt I needed to get started as a filmmaker.

What attracted you to the topic of *Scumbling*?

It was autobiographical. You're supposed to make films about something you know. I knew my own story, I knew about my struggles with my family, with having a breakdown and recovering in my parents' house and wanting to be an artist and trying to get myself together to take that next step. That was a no-brainer, to make that the subject of my film. I also wanted to make a feature but I knew I couldn't jump into a feature film yet, and that making a short would give me a lot of practice to warm up to a feature.

Before you shot a single scene, what were the first things you did to get up and running?

I had to have a script. I didn't know much about screenwriting at that time, but I managed to get my script together and it kept evolving right up until the shoot. Also, a big priority for me was finding the right actors. I went through some discouraging experiences in the beginning auditioning actors who did not work out — one actor for the lead fell through at the last minute when I was doing a pilot — and I was determined to do it differently next time. I was going to make finding that right lead actor my priority, and I did. I went to New York and I was able to get access to the Stella Adler Studio and I got a great leading actress named Mary Kickel. That was a huge priority for me because I knew that was the key to the film working.

Did you have a budget? Did you do any fundraising?

My associate producer helped me fundraise. We had a couple of fundraising events and we made invitations and invited people to two events and solicited through letters and mailing. In the end I used a lot of my own money as well.

What was the biggest unforeseen problem?

I had all of my locations set up, and two days before the shoot I went over to one of the locations. I had a pro-choice sticker on the back of my car, and when I went to the door, the owner said, "We aren't interested anymore. We don't want to do it." They didn't like my politics. So, I had to hustle around and find a new exterior which I did.

How long did the project take you and was it longer or shorter than you expected?

Maybe about a year and a half to do the whole thing. I really didn't know how long it would take but it wasn't a huge issue because it got done.

How many film festivals did you submit to and how many did you get into?

I got into two or three and got turned down by at least 25.

What did you learn from the film festival process?

I think one reason was because it was an awkward length. When I first made the film it was 34 minutes, and that was really a bad length. It needed to be shorter. When I finally went back and re-edited I cut out five minutes. Now I think if I were entering it into a festival it would be much more viable because it would be under a half hour. The timing was a little draggy and just needed to be tightened up. Those were things I did later.

What was your most memorable or enjoyable moment during this whole process?

When I showed the film to my family, and it was a film that was very autobiographical, my brother said, "I felt like you recreated my whole life just as it was." I was so moved by what he said, because that's really what I was trying to do.

What advice would you give a new filmmaker getting ready to tackle their first project?

The most important thing is love what you are doing. Love your story and love the process because that has to feed you during all of that long and sometimes frustrating period of making the film and bringing it to life. ◆

P. Edward Claypoole & Rip Saling

THE ONE PERCENT: THE MARK HIMEBAUGH
STORY (2016) | DOCUMENTARY

Synopsis: On November 25, 1991, 11-year-old Mark Himebaugh disappeared from his Del Haven home in New Jersey. He has been missing since.

Was there a specific time in your life when you realized that you wanted to be a filmmaker?

RIP: When I moved to LA in my twenties I worked for Artist Management Group, so I got to see the management side of film. Then I went into production and learned that side of things. After some time I decided this is what suited me best.

ED: Ever since I began watching movies, I just knew it was something that I wanted to be involved in. I eventually went on to get a degree in video production and have been working in the field ever since.

Did you go to school for film or video production, and was it what you expected it to be?

RIP: No, I have no formal training in film or video production.

ED: I have a degree in video production from The Art Institute of Philadelphia; unfortunately the school no longer exists. It was more of a trade school, very hands on, which I enjoyed, and they really allowed you to be creative. I was never the school type of person, so this was a great fit for me. I never thought I would graduate college, so getting an Associate's Degree was good enough for me.

What attracted you to the topic of *The One Percent: The Mark Himebaugh Story*?

RIP: When Ed and I were discussing different ideas, and possibly working on a project together, we came up with the idea for this documentary, because it was and still is an unsolved case. It was also close to our family since our uncle Joe dated Mark's mother, Maureen, for decades until his passing in 2019. We were hoping to shed light and open new doors on the case, possibly finding some answers for Maureen and her family.

ED: Out of all of the ideas we had discussed, this was by far the one we had a true passion for. It is an open case and its close to our family. We really wanted to tell this story the right way, because we wanted it to be a happy story, a story celebrating his life, but also a story that seeks resolution, because there isn't a day that goes by that Maureen doesn't think about her son.

Before you shot a single scene, what were the first things you did to get up and running?

RIP: We wanted to figure out the right way of telling the story, which was from Mark's childhood all the way until the day he went missing. We did a lot of research specifically on the day he disappeared and what was done and wasn't done during the investigation.

ED: We also came up with an outline of the documentary from start to finish, and followed that as best as we could. We researched a lot of former investigators and a volunteer who helped look for Mark when he went missing. We spent a lot of time reading old news articles looking for anyone we could talk to.

Did you have a budget? Did you do any fundraising?

RIP: We did very minimal fundraising and that was just used for TV news footage.

ED: We raised $3,000 from a GoFundMe campaign. We chose $3,000 because that was exactly how much we needed for news footage and b-roll. We got footage from HBO Sports, ABC News in Philadelphia and we got footage and stock photos from various sites online. With HBO and NBC, the minimum amount of footage we could buy was 30 seconds; we could choose any 30 seconds we wanted and the cost was $1,000. So for the both we were able to get one minute for $2,000. The remaining was used on various websites getting different types of b-roll.

What was the biggest unforeseen problem?

RIP: Because this is an open investigation, the current detectives would not provide answers or interviews on this case. We also weren't given access to some pieces of evidence in the case because they were concerned that we could jeopardize the ongoing investigation. We were only allowed to talk to previous/retired detectives and anyone else we could find on our own.

ED: On a technical side, we had some snags with editing and sound. We had to make adjustments to make things work. Not every shoot went perfectly, but we were both able to make changes on the fly which made our lives easier in the end.

How long did the project take you and was it longer or shorter than you expected?

RIP: It took two years to complete this project but I kind of feel like if we wanted to, we could keep working with it, maybe do a full feature at some point.

ED: When we first sat down, I was expecting it to take 2–3 years because nothing ever goes according to plan. We did finish in just under two, so that was extremely satisfying.

How many film festivals did you submit to and how many did you get into?

RIP: I personally think we should have gotten into more, but everybody feels that way when it's their project and they are extremely passionate about it. I just wish more people could have seen it.

ED: We submitted to 18 and got into two. One of the festivals we got into was The Cape May Film Festival in southern New Jersey. That meant a lot to us because that's where he went missing. There were a lot of people that showed up to see our documentary there.

What did you learn from the film festival process?

RIP: To be honest, I didn't learn much about it. I was happy we made it into The Cape May Film Festival. I think the most important thing was we got in there, and the story was told again down there, where it happened. I really don't understand though how the process works or who decides.

ED: I was surprised that we only got into two, but I did learn a lot, and I learned a lot more about the film festival side while writing this book.

What was your most memorable or enjoyable moment during this whole process?

RIP: Being at The Cape May Film Festival with our family and friends. Maureen and Mark's brother, Matt, were there, along with one of the detectives who helped us with the documentary. Being able to watch it with her was important.

ED: I would agree. Maureen had told us right before the screening that she hadn't seen it. We had sent her multiple copies but she was waiting for a special time, when our whole family could get together to watch it. When she found out we got into the festival she said she decided to wait until then. So after the film ended and the lights came on it was a pile of emotions. Some people were clapping, others were crying, but we got to be there with Maureen and Matt when they first saw it. Even though it is a sad subject, we really put our hearts into this, and we think it showed and it made our families proud.

What advice would you give a new filmmaker getting ready to tackle their first project?

RIP: You have to be passionate about the subject, because ultimately, you're doing something that is not paying you. You need to know what story you want to tell, and you have to be willing to dive in 100%.

ED: Find a story that you love. Something you can't stop thinking about, and then figure out how to tell it in your own way. Be willing to make mistakes, but learn from those mistakes. Take anything you can get for free — people are always willing to help — but always be willing to repay the favor. I've built a few good relationships over the years where I know I can call certain people and they will drop what they are doing to help me, knowing if they call me the next week I will do the same. Always ask questions, because you never know where they might lead you. And last, stop thinking about it and just go out and do it. ◆

Nancy Schwartzman

ROLL RED ROLL 2018 | DOCUMENTARY

Synopsis: At a 2012 pre-season high school football party in Steubenville, Ohio, a young woman is raped. The aftermath exposes an entire culture of complicity and the roles that peer pressure, denial, sports machismo, and social media played in the tragedy.

Was there a specific time in your life when you realized that you wanted to be a filmmaker?

It was probably my senior year of college. I had always loved movies, and I remember early on when I would help my mom empty groceries from her car, there would be this magazine, kind of like *TV Guide,* but they would review movies, and I remember reading all of those reviews and I would gobble that up. At the time I didn't imagine that I would grow up to make movies. Jump to my senior year in college. I was doing a lot of street photography, and loved talking to people, so I would write a small essay about them so you could hear their voices and really get into their lives. It wasn't until a few years later when I was 24 that I actually bought my first camera and started filming.

Did you go to school for film or video production, and was it what you expected it to be?

No I did not go to film school. I had to learn production by doing. I think, especially in documentary filmmaking, a lot of us learn on our own and we come in from different areas.

What attracted you to the topic of *Roll Red Roll*?

Youth culture, technology and sexuality have been my area of focus for a very long time so this felt very natural. I didn't realize that I was stepping into the genre of true crime and when I first started this project, it wasn't as big as a genre as it is now.

Before you shot a single scene, what were the first things you did to get up and running?

I did a lot of research online about the case: who was important, who were the players, who were the characters I wanted to find. I was really trying to understand from afar the ecosystem: who did what, who revealed what, who trusts who. I made a phone call to Alex Goddard to see if she would talk to me; she wound up becoming my main protagonist. I did an initial call to see what she was like and most importantly, if she would trust me. Before even shooting a single scene, I went out there to see the town to figure out what it was like. Is there a story here? It was basically a research and development trip.

Did you have a budget? Did you do any fundraising?

I did not do online crowd fundraising because the film was sensitive. I couldn't be public with the fact that I'm making a film about a crime that no one wants to talk about. I applied for a little bit of money for my research and development trip, and once I got started I began writing grants and looking for funding that way.

What was the biggest unforeseen problem?

There were so many problems. The first types of problems were that people said they would talk to me, and as I began shaping my film around them, they would change their mind. There were also issues with legal rights to fair use. We thought we could use all these leaked documents because they were made public, they were online and on Twitter. So we cut some into our trailer and then we learned later that we couldn't do that, you can't just grab anything from the internet and throw it on TV. If you want to use it, you have to argue a case for fair use. So I learned a lot about intellectual property and fair use rights.

How long did the project take you and was it longer or shorter than you expected?

Initially I thought I was going to make a short film, but the movie began growing more and more, and I realized it couldn't be a short anymore. I began filming in August 2013 and we finished the film in December 2017. With the release of the film it was a total of five years from start to finish.

How many film festivals did you submit to and how many did you get into?

I don't know the exact number but I think it's around 40.

What did you learn from the film festival process?

I think the whole festival strategy really depends on the type of film you have. For me, I was able to test my film in different parts of the country and see how it played. A film about Ohio, rape culture and football is going to play one way in New York City as opposed to playing in Columbus. I feel like it's a tour, you get to travel and meet audiences. I showed my film six times in the Czech Republic. While I was there, I also attended a few educational screenings of it, and these Czech teenagers were so horrified by my film; they couldn't understand why American kids would treat each other so horribly. I showed it in Mexico and the reaction was, "We don't have football, we have soccer, but we deal with the same problems here." I also had the chance to go to China and they translated the film to *Evil Little Town* and I thought that was the best title ever. It was great going to other countries and seeing the audiences' reactions. It was extremely valuable to me.

What was your most memorable or enjoyable moment during this process?

My premier was the most memorable. It was amazing to share the film publicly for the first time on a big screen in a packed theatre, to bring Alex and Rachel who were in the film to the front of the theatre for a standing ovation. People kept telling me to enjoy the premier, there is only one, and I never really knew what they meant until that night, and it was really amazing.

What advice would you give a new filmmaker getting ready to tackle their first project?

With nonfiction you better love your story because you're going to live with it forever. You're going to know those people. They are always going to be a part of your life. You're going to hold enormous responsibility, because its nonfiction, to all the people that you document, and it's going to take longer than you expected it to. There's also something great about not having a clue about what you're getting into, because if you did, you may not do it. ◆

Kelly Murray

THE ASTRONOMER (2016) | DRAMA/FANTASY

Synopsis: In 1916, a young woman sneaks out of her astronomy class to explore the night sky with a band of mystical gypsies. She comes to discover that she learns more about the universe outside in the world than she ever could inside the classroom.

Was there a specific time in your life when you realized that you wanted to be a filmmaker?

I wouldn't say that there was one specific moment, but I have always been fascinated with film and movies. At a young age, I loved stories — books, television, film — and loved to draw, perform, sing, etc. I think having that creative streak and an active imagination, I gravitated toward pursuing a creative career path. I first wanted to be an actress, and I did a little theatre in high school and college, but I never pursued it. I focused on creative writing and I eventually found my strength in storytelling behind the camera.

Did you go to school for film or video production, and was it what you expected it to be?

I did not. I went to the University of Delaware and I majored in English and history. My first office job out of college was in marketing for a small recruiting company. We were exploring using video in our marketing efforts, and I expressed my interest in filmmaking. At the time, the CEO's colleague, an independent filmmaker, was using the office as a location for a pickup shoot and I asked to shadow him on set. After that experience, I was hooked. From there, I started applying to film jobs in the area, learning as I went, and understanding the methodology of production. I did anything I felt I was qualified for. I started out as a production assistant, and then started getting jobs in the Art Department doing hair, makeup, costuming. I eventually worked my way up to production management roles. I made a lot of connections in the Philadelphia and West Chester areas of Pennsylvania.

What attracted you to the topic of *The Astronomer*?

The Astronomer was a blend of timing. I had been involved in a lot of independent films in the area, and I was itching to make something of my own. I saw a call for artists at The Delaware Contemporary in Wilmington, asking for video exhibits. The theme was outer space exploration. I had read a poem a few weeks earlier called "When I Heard the Learn'd Astronomer" by Walt Whitman, so it was fresh in my mind. Inspired by the poem and the exhibit theme, I wrote a short script which emerged as a film adaptation of the Walt Whitman poem. I wanted to stay true to the era of the poem, while incorporating some bohemian fantasy themes that were prevalent during the early 20th century, so I set the film in 1916. Looking back, it was ambitious to do a period film as my very first film, but it came together really well.

Before you shot a single scene, what were the first things you did to get up and running?

We had a really tight pre-production phase because we were under the museum's deadline. I am a planner and I believe that all of the hard work is done in pre-production. The more thorough your pre-production is, the easier you can execute once you get to filming. Once the script was complete, I chose which shooting locations I wanted to use. Then my Director of Photography, Hillary Hanak, and I developed a shot list for each scene. Since this was a period piece, we had to find costumes for the film which we found at thrift shops. We sourced all of the props and created costume pieces in my living room. It was extremely fun going around looking for these things, and being able to use local resources.

Did you have a budget? Did you do any fundraising?

No, we did not have a fixed budget and we did not do any fundraising. At the time, we just purchased what we needed. We kept track of everything, but there was no set budget. Since this was my first film project, our crew and talent were volunteers. The biggest expenses were food, props and costumes. The estimated total costs from pre-production to post-production were $1,200.

What was the biggest unforeseen problem?

During the first day of the shoot, our makeup artist called out sick. We were getting the talent ready to start filming when we got the news. Fortunately, I had makeup available and wound up doing it myself. Since the film had fantasy elements that relied heavily on talent being in makeup and costuming, not having a dedicated makeup artist on set felt like a major roadblock, but in the end, it forced us to get creative. It wound up working out for the best.

How long did the project take you and was it longer or shorter than you expected?

It took three to four weeks of planning. We shot for two days on a weekend, and then one pickup day. In total it took about three months from beginning to final picture.

How many film festivals did you submit to and how many did you get into?

We submitted to 10 to 15 festivals. The film was accepted into The Women's Film Festival, The Media Film Festival, The Jim Thorpe Film Festival and The Playhouse West Film Festival. At the time, my main focus was getting into the museum exhibit because that's what brought this whole thing to fruition. Once we got into the exhibit, we decided to explore the film festival circuit.

What did you learn from the film festival process?

The film festival experience was positive. It was all extremely new to me, so I was excited to be able to attend the festivals and share my work. We had approached the making of the film with a two-part strategy: if we didn't get accepted into the museum exhibit, we would still have a film that we could submit to festivals. So, the film festival process felt like an added bonus. During the process, I learned how expensive submissions can be. We were submitting to all different kinds of festivals. Since then, I've become more strategic with my film festival approach. It's important to consider regional festivals, genre-specific festivals or if the festival has an overarching theme.

What was your most memorable or enjoyable moment during this process?

I have two memorable moments from the making of *The Astronomer*. After we had set up the first shot and I had the realization that we were actually making it, that the film had come alive off of the pages of my script, and I could see my vision becoming a reality — that was really rewarding. Secondly, seeing the audiences' reactions at our film premiere in West Chester and the film festivals was really remarkable. Knowing that the story had an emotional impact on so many people was really fulfilling.

What advice would you give a new filmmaker getting ready to tackle their first project?

If there's a story you want to tell, make it yourself. Just do it. Write your script, pick up a camera and just go for it. I think one of the reasons *The Astronomer* got done was because we just went for it. We didn't second-guess ourselves and were present during the process. Secondly, find people to collaborate with that you trust and that will challenge you. ◆

Don Argott

ROCK SCHOOL (2005) | DOCUMENTARY

Synopsis: At the real life School of Rock a group of misfit kids get in touch with their inner rock star.

Was there a specific time in your life when you realized that you wanted to be a filmmaker?

Growing up, I was drawn to early rock and heavy metal and because of that I always thought I wanted to be in a band. That was the first thing that I became very passionate about and that I saw myself doing to make a living. At the same time, my parents were big into video rentals and we would rent movies every three to four days. From that point on, movies became a big part of my life. I specifically remember seeing *Goodfellas* on VHS and seeing the overhead shot where Joe Pesci is killed … that shot did something to me; it opened me up to look at films differently. I started consuming all those late 70s filmmakers like Coppola, Scorsese and Kubrick. I would watch them specifically to break down shots and see how they were framed. I wound up giving up on the career of being in a successful band and focused on film instead.

Did you go to school for film or video production, and was it what you expected it to be?

I grew up in northern New Jersey, and after graduating high school I started dating a girl who was going to Villanova University, so I started coming up to Pennsylvania to visit her. I had never really spent any time in Philadelphia before, but I really got taken by the place. So I started looking at schools and found The Art Institute of Philadelphia, which offered music engineering and film programs. It was all hands-on which was perfect for me; I don't do well with things like theory. I felt very fortunate to be at that school at that time when things were shifting from analog over to digital. It was the perfect program for me and I'm really grateful for that experience at the school.

What attracted you to the topic of *Rock School*?

It was really the perfect blend of all of my interests growing up. This sounds like it was out of a movie but I would walk around the city and I would see all of these pasted posters of the Paul Greene School of Rock Music. These posters would say, "The Paul Greene School of Rock does the music of The Who or The Paul Greene School of Rock does the music of Metallica." And I would think, "What is this? I bet it would make an amazing documentary." I got his information and reached out to him and told him what I wanted to do, and by the end of the week I started shooting the movie. With my background in music and then my background in production, it was just this perfect moment of putting all of that together and taking that step forward with this film. It was the perfect film for me on so many levels. It opened up a lot of doors and really started my career.

Before you shot a single scene, what were the first things you did to get up and running?

When I got to the point where I was going to do this film, I was confident in the fact that I could shoot the whole thing myself without a crew; I could shoot it, direct it, do sound and cut it. That was my plan going forward to keep costs down and make this film a reality. At that point I was into a lot of documentaries, specifically a documentary called *American Movie*, which I credit for getting me into documentaries.. It was the first time I had seen a doc that made me laugh out loud. Up to that point I always thought documentaries were those boring things they showed you in school. I watched that movie super critically and analyzed how they crafted it, and I tried to figure out how to tell my story using a real person and situation. I would say that was most of my prep and the rest was just going into the school and pointing a camera, and trying to tell what the school was and what it was about. It was just the perfect moment for me and the beginning of my career.

Did you have a budget? Did you do any fundraising?

We did not have a budget when we started the film. The majority of the shooting didn't cost a whole lot because I had all of the equipment, I wasn't hiring anyone, it was just all of my time. We were fortunate enough to be able to film everything on a super low budget.

What was the biggest unforeseen problem?

The music licensing. Although the production costs were kept low, the kids were playing Black Sabbath, Santana, Frank Zappa and Van Halen, and we were really unprepared for what that was going to look like, and what it would take to clear the music. We had to have those hard discussions when we had a scene where the musician wouldn't license us the music, or what they are asking for to include it in the film didn't make sense, and we had to cut the scene or replace it with another song we could license.

How long did the project take you and was it longer or shorter than you expected?

Because it was my first film, there was very little expectation. We had filmed for less than a year, probably about nine months. It was always just that thing that we were doing, but at the same time we were running a business, so we worked on it when we had time. There was no set in stone schedule. We worked on it as a labor of love.

How many film festivals did you submit to and how many did you get into?

One of the first things we did, which doesn't even exist anymore, was that we submitted to the IFP (Independent Feature Production) in NYC with a work in progress. Back then it could be a rough cut, short or selected scenes that you got to show to industry professionals. We submitted and got in using 14 minutes of footage of selected scenes from the film. We showed our footage, did a little question and answer following, and right after we were approached by all of these companies like Sony, Miramax and HBO. Everybody was handing us their cards and asking us to send them the final product. We wound up getting a sales agent, Cinetic Media, and they helped guide us through the film festival world.

What did you learn from the film festival process?

It's exciting being a part of it, but it's also terrifying. It's kind of like being at a casino, you're either going to win or you're going to lose and the stakes are really high. You put a lot of time and effort into this movie you made and now you are showing it to people, but you're not just hoping they like it; you want them to buy it, to believe in it. So there can be a lot of stress, but the stress is also being felt by your peers — filmmakers you meet along the way — which is also exciting. There is a lot of camaraderie. It was such a huge part of our early career.

What was your most memorable or enjoyable moment during this whole process?

One specific moment that stands out is once we had sold it at the LA Film Festival, New Market had done a special screening at the 2005 Sundance Film Festival. They didn't ask for any changes to the actual film, the only thing they really wanted to do was push the soundtrack, and they asked if we could tack on an end credits sequence. So they wound up getting Alice Cooper to do "Schools Out" with the kids. So after the screening at Sundance there was an event afterwards where Alice Cooper played with the kids and we filmed it and put it in as the end credit sequence. At the end of the night when everything was done, I walked up on the stage by myself and thought about this whole journey I had been on and how I wound up getting here. It was really a special moment.

What advice would you give a new filmmaker getting ready to tackle their first project?

Filmmaking in general is figuring out how to overcome a series of endless obstacles. It's all of the cliché things you always hear but the most important thing is to never give up. If you believe in it, you have to see it through. When it looks like the odds are against you and all signs are pointing you to throw your hands up in the air and walk away, you have to push through it. You have to believe in yourself. ◆

Demian Lichtenstein

3000 MILES TO GRACELAND (2001) | ACTION/COMEDY

Synopsis: A gang of ex-cons rob a casino during Elvis convention week.

Was there a specific time in your life when you realized that you wanted to be a filmmaker?

There are three pivotal moments. When I was eight years old, my mother Fonda — a creator, artist and teacher — had a Canon 35mm still camera. At the time we lived in Temple Hill, Vermont. In the fall, Vermont is one of the most beautiful places on the planet. We went for a walk one day down this old dirt road that had pine needles all over it and maple trees on each side. It was beautiful with the fall foliage, blue skies and puffy white clouds. We climbed and sat on top of this mountain that overlooked the Broodbrook Valley, and my mother engaged me in a photo lesson. She had me put in the film and then asked me to pick a lens. This, as a filmmaker and director, was a pivotal point in my life, because she had explained to me what the difference was between an 18mm, 24mm, 35mm and 85mm lens. At the time I chose an 85mm lens, put it on the camera and started looking through it. I began focusing on apple trees, a rock wall, pine trees, clouds and some deer walking by. I took my eye away from the lens without taking a shot and my mom could see that I had gotten upset and she asked me what was wrong. I said I didn't know which picture to take, and she asked why, to which I replied that, "They are all so beautiful; what if I take the wrong one?" There was this moment of silence and my mom looked at me and said, "I understand, but I'm going to teach you something and you have to make sure you remember this for the rest of your life. It's just as important, perhaps even more so, what you leave out of your frame as what you put in your frame." I thought about it and watched my mom turn her head to look at the clouds and I picked up the camera and took a picture of her face; that was my first real photograph. That was all that was in the picture. I went on to take many more because my mother reminded me that there were 34 pictures left on the film. I learned that day that it wasn't about just the first take; you have multiple takes. For me, understanding about the relationship to the frame, the relationship to the lens, the relationship to light and what types of different glass lenses, that all happened in that particular moment.

The second moment was when I was an avid model builder; I loved to build dioramas. I would get a piece of plywood and fill it with dirt, make a river, build a little farmhouse, a Panzer tank, an American P51 Mustang … I would heat up my exacto blade and put bullet holes on the side of the plane and I would spray paint cotton to make it look like explosions; I was really into the detail of the image I was creating. I would spend weeks building these things, doing chores to get money so I could go out and buy these models to build. Once they were completed I would eventually get bored with it, so I would empty out shotgun shells to get the gunpowder and make little bombs, dowse it with lighter fluid and then set it on fire and blow it up. After doing this multiple times, my mother showed me a Bell & Howell Super 8 video camera, especially the zoom lens, and said, "I know you're going to build another diorama and blow it up, but I want you far away zoomed in on the explosions, this way I won't have to spend the evening taking plastic out of your face and worrying that you're going to go blind. From now on, any time you're going to blow something up, you need to film it, and stand far away." This was the start of my action career of filming blowing up the things that I built.

The third moment was when I got the opportunity to work on a movie set. My mom, who worked for the Vermont Council of the Arts, had some state-approval over movie productions, and got me an internship on *The Man That Corrupted Hadleyburg* starring Fred Gwynne (better known as Herman Munster). I couldn't believe I was on this set working with him. This was a real Hollywood movie. The circus came to town and I left with it. I realized then that this was what I was going to do with the rest of my life.

Did you go to school for film or video production, and was it what you expected it to be?

Everything that I have done has been a class in filmmaking. On *The Man That Corrupted Hadleyburg* I worked in every department on the film crew as an intern. I eventually moved to New York City where I went to The High School of Art & Design. I wound up studying film and the first three years were pretty much the equivalent of going to any college program for the same education. I graduated on stage at Carnegie Hall in 1984 with the NYC Media Award for the top film and television high school student in the city. I received the Helena Rubinstein scholarship which was a work study scholarship at New York University where I majored in film and television at the Tisch School of the Arts. I wound up winning the best action film while in school at the Tisch School of the Arts Film Festival. While in school, I started my production company, Lightstone, which I still have today. In my senior year of college my father gave me the option of getting a new car or a 16mm Arriflex film camera. I chose the camera.

What attracted you to the topic of *3000 Miles to Graceland*?

I had been working on another script written by Richie Recco, my co-screenwriter on *3000 Miles to Graceland*, called Brooklyn Fiasco. At this point I had already written, produced and directed my first indie full feature film called *Low Ball* and so I was looking to make my second film. We talked quite often about Brooklyn Fiasco and out of those conversations, *3000 Miles to Graceland* was born. Richie wrote a great draft and from there we worked on the script and kept refining it over time. I decided to pack up my bags and drive cross country to Los Angeles with the intent of raising money to make this film. We were originally looking at making it as an indie picture for around 8-10 million dollars. But through a series of great events, I ended up pitching the project to Kevin Costner and he signed on after reading the script. I was friends with Goldie Hawn at the time, and Kurt Russell wound up reading it and also signed on. With these two actors on board, the money came together very quickly and Warner Brothers signed on as a distributor and we were off making a movie. It happened less than a year from the first day I set foot in Los Angeles.

Before you shot a single scene, what were the first things you did to get up and running?

There are hundreds of things a person does when prepping for a movie. One of the first things I did while working on the film was to create a look book; a visual representation of what the film should look like. Is it bright and poppy and pretty? Is it dark and misty and foreboding? What images and angles are you looking for? I prefer drawing and painting, so early on I hired concept artists to do some work on what the characters might look like, and some of the iconic images for the film. I used this book of original art when I pitched the idea to Kevin Costner.

I also go through the script with colored pencils and pens, scene by scene, to make notes on each shot; from here to here its low angle, from here to here its worm's eye view. I will walk through the entire script and write down what I visually see and how that relates to the position of the camera and the type of lens I want to use. This can take days to weeks. That is a critical part for me. I then go back through it drawing my scratchy, not so great, thumbnail storyboards. What does this scene look like to me?

Then I go back and start numbering the shots and at the same time draw up floor plans. I place my camera in the floor plan and I block out the scenes. One of the things the floor plan really helps reveal is that shot one, three, seven and 14 are all from the same exact angle and camera position. When you want to move quickly on a set, in principle once you set a camera somewhere and get the lighting right, you want to get every possible shot you can from where that camera is. Once you move that camera, going back to that same position and getting everything right is extremely difficult. So with the floor plan on top of having a shot list, you now have a shot sequence.

For me I think directors need to have three basic key ingredients. First, their entire job is to drive the story forward in the most efficient manner they can. Second, as a filmmaker you need to have the base technical knowledge and understanding of what a camera is, the different ways you can hold and move it and what the lenses are you have to play with. Third is leadership, that you have done enough internal work on yourself, so that as the director of this film, you have the capacity to lead the actors and crew. This is critical because you need people to trust you as you lead them through this process.

Did you have a budget? Did you do any fundraising?

When we originally started our intent was to make the movie for 8-10 million. The budget number shifted and changed considerably over time. The final budget came in at 50 million dollars.

What was the biggest unforeseen problem?

There were several. We had an accident on the set that landed four of my actors and two of my crew in the emergency room. I had to shut down the movie, and I planted myself in the hospital and I didn't leave until about 18 hours later when every single cast and crew member had been treated and released from the hospital. At this point, I thought not only was my movie over; I thought my entire film career was over. The following day, all of the actors and crew members showed up with stitches and bandages and said, "Let's get to work." I was told later that it was my commitment and compassion for the people that were injured that had everybody show up to continue working on the film.

How long did the project take you and was it longer or shorter than you expected?

From conception to completion it was really fast; it was just over two years.

How many movie theatres was this distributed to and what did you learn from the mass distribution process?

We went into 3,000 theatres. I learned that marketing the movie you made, rather than a movie that people want to try to sell, is one of the most critical things you can do. In other words, I made a gritty, violent, in-your-face action film with an American hero (Kevin Costner), playing against type as a pretty evil guy. The original trailer that I cut was to a Chemical Brothers song; a hard, cutting-edge track. The studio opted to cut a trailer that was a happy go lucky comedy about Elvis with a ZZ Top song, Viva Las Vegas, that isn't even in my movie. The film is a dark comedy but the studio marketed and prepped it as a light happy-go-lucky action comedy. That's not the movie I made.

What was your most memorable or enjoyable moment during this whole process?

One of the most memorable moments that I always think about is when we were shooting the big warehouse combat shootout sequence. We were crushed on time and schedule, and the only way to really get everything done was to have three entire units shooting at the same time. The way it worked was I was getting close-ups with the actors with action and explosions going on in the background. Most of the second unit action was being directed by the second unit director, which included gunfire and big explosions. The third unit was shooting all the lead up shots, police cars arriving to the scene and SWAT setting off flash bangs and running through smoke. I had a break from the action, so I walked over to the biggest set. I stepped underneath the yellow caution tape and began checking out the set. A second later I got a rough tap on my shoulder and I turned around to a gentleman scolding me for ignoring the tape. I had no idea who he was and he had no idea who I was. I stepped behind the tape and that's when I knew that I had arrived in a space in time where the thing I was creating was bigger than me. This was a great teachable moment for me, it taught me how to be humble.

What advice would you give a new filmmaker getting ready to tackle their first project?

If there is anything else in the world that you would rather do, go do that instead. For filmmaking specifically, you must be prepared to sacrifice everything you have to fulfill your vision; that could be relationships with family and friends or even your integrity. If you are going to be a filmmaker and you are going to make your first film, give everything you have to that, knowing that you are going to be sacrificing many things along the way that other people will not or would not sacrifice in order to complete your vision and bring it to the screen. Be clear to yourself that this is what you want to do and never quit. ◆

Stuart Connelly

THE SUSPECT (2014) | THRILLER

Synopsis: When two African American social scientists pose as bank robbers in an effort to understand the racial dynamics of small-town law enforcement, their experiment takes an unplanned, deadly turn.

Was there a specific time in your life when you realized that you wanted to be a filmmaker?

When I was a kid — this'll date me a little bit — I made Super 8mm movies, so I knew I wanted to be a filmmaker when I was very young. Then I went to film school, but it didn't gel with me because I started really understanding the complexities of what it would take to bring a film to life. I looked at the whole process and realized that if I wanted to be a director, I would have to start as a PA and worm my way through this entire complex business system, and from my perspective it seemed that the amount of time and effort it would take was too daunting. I refocused my education on writing, because I looked at writing as something that you were in charge of; there was no space between you and the final product. So I spent about 15 years as a writer in various incarnations and left film behind … except as a fan.

Did you go to school for film or video production, and was it what you expected it to be?

I went to Newhouse School for film at Syracuse University, the school of public communications. I started out in film and then wound up majoring in journalism with a minor in film. My thought at the time was maybe I'll eventually go into advertising or something like that with my background in film. But I didn't spend time in production at school. From that standpoint, I'm completely self-taught. Which means, of course, I studied the movies.

What attracted you to the topic of *The Suspect*?

I had written a book in 2011 called *Behind the Dream* about the 1963
March on Washington with Martin Luther King's personal lawyer and
speechwriter Clarence B. Jones. In the process of getting to know Clarence
and hearing his stories, I became more and more interested in the Civil
Rights Movement. I watched the trajectory of the book, hoping the film/
TV rights would get optioned. But that didn't happen, and in fact while the
book was well-reviewed it didn't crack any bestseller lists. After the book
came out, I asked myself what my next career move would be, considering
I now had a track record as a historian writing about African American
issues. I could write another book in that world somewhere. Or, could
I reach a larger audience by making a film around those same issues?
I started tinkering with a thriller that addressed the African American
struggle in a way I thought topical, interesting, accessible and surprising.
Clarence is well known in the African American community and I'd met
a lot of his friends, including a famous actor who wanted to play Clarence
in a biopic. This actor asked me to write a script based on Clarence's life.
Even though that project never went forward, I built a good relationship
with this actor and I shared my script *The Suspect* with him. It excited
him and he committed to the project. That laid the groundwork for my
directorial debut.

Before you shot a single scene, what were the first things you did to get up and running?

I had written the script in my very small town and I had used actual
locations as descriptions for places in my script. It was very helpful for me
to go park in front of a bank or in front of a motel and write about locations
as I actually saw them. I never thought I'd end up shooting it here. But as
the project came together, in the back of my mind I started wondering if
it actually made sense to use the locations I'd scripted. I saw the film in a
very particular way — I used Gregory Crewdson photographs and Edward
Hopper paintings as the visual guideposts, and I realized I didn't want to
do the LA version of this thriller. That helped us imagine the budget better,
and the hometown advantage helped to offset some of the concern investors
always have, reasonably, about a first-time director.

Did you have a budget? Did you do any fundraising?

A very careful budget. That's a must, and budgeting's a skill unto itself. At the time, as I said, I had an actor attached who was in the public eye. He loved the script, and he convinced another well-known actor to come aboard. We put together an investor package with the script, my book, the budget and the letters of intent that said these two planned to star. It didn't take too many meetings to raise the financing. People believed in the project, but it was more than just the script; the package made it seem more … possible, I suppose. More real. It's interesting; at the end of the day, neither of those actors ended up making the film, which is just the logistics of scheduling in Hollywood. But with our incredible investors' backing, the project was a go, and we were, by the time of casting, in a new position. We went from beggars to choosers. A go-project is a game changer — we were able to reach incredible actors who we had no previous relationship with. We were offering actors jobs, rather than hyping a possibility.

What was the biggest unforeseen problem?

Probably the logistics of shooting one very complicated scene, a critical point of the story, that takes place on a mountainside. There's a car that's gone over a cliff and its hanging on the edge of this precipice and the people at the top have to repel down and recover something from this car. So you have the mountainside, the car at a precarious angle, actors inching down on ropes to get to this car, and on top of everything else, the thing catches fire. When you see all these other movies that have huge budgets, they're able to do anything with CGI or green screen, but we had to do 99% of the work in camera to sell this complicated illusion. All of this is really easy to imagine but on a limited budget we didn't know how we were going to do it. We actually wound up renting a truck repair facility that had 40-foot ceilings that allowed us to build the mountain from scratch. It was extremely complicated to do but we pulled it off and when you watch the movie it feels real. The fact that we did it with such limited resources is a tribute to my production designer and the way we were able to communicate.

How long did the project take you and was it longer or shorter than you expected?

I think it took about two years from the story idea to the finished, locked picture. It actually went very fast. There was a lot of paperwork between the promise of financing and having money in the bank to make our offers to cast, but when you do make those offers, they have to include a specific window of production time. So you plant your flag on your shooting schedule with that first offer, then it just comes down to lining everyone and everything in that window and getting it shot. Post-production was rushed because the production had a tax rebate through the state, and in order to receive it the movie had to be done by the end of the calendar year. So the whole post-production process was very fast.

How many film festivals did you submit to and how many did you get in?

The calendar works around January and Sundance — everybody knows that Sundance is the premiere event for independent film. If you get in there you're golden and then every other festival starts coming after you. If that doesn't work, there are other big ones like Toronto, Venice, Tribeca, Berlin, but everyone aims at Sundance. The submission deadline is October and we were just finishing filming — we didn't have a completed film, so instead we submitted a work in progress. And we actually heard from them — they sent an email and asked for an updated version as soon as possible, which was the best festival news I had ever received at that point in my career. We celebrated that achievement and were hopeful we might be invited to Sundance, but we wound up not getting selected. Because of *The Suspect's* subject matter, the next festival on our radar was the American Black Film Festival, which we got into. Once that happened we began discussions with a company about distribution. At the same time, we decided to slow down the festival submission process, but we started getting requests to show our film at different festivals. Because I was new to the filmmaking world, I didn't quite understand why we were getting these requests, but I learned that film festivals are always looking at other film festivals to see what's hot. I think we wound up getting into about 18 or 19.

What did you learn from the film festival process?

Just like any other Hollywood story, access at the highest levels has a lot to do with connections. There are producers that I know where it seems any film they make, it's Sundance-ready and practically pre-approved. From the outside, applying to these festivals, you feel like you are entering a real competition where the best will get picked, yet that is not necessarily the case. Which is disappointing. The other thing is, many festivals often have an unspoken theme, and if you fit into the theme that year, you have a better chance of getting in even if your film isn't necessarily the best of the crop. You can't always have your heart set on getting into Sundance or this festival or that festival. It is an extremely convoluted process. The good news is that there are more opportunities for distribution than ever before, so the festival anointing isn't quite as important for indie film these days.

What was your most memorable or enjoyable moment during this whole process?

Our DIT handed me dailies on DVD every day and I hated watching them, because I knew exactly what we'd shot; what I cared about was how those takes would work with other angles I shot. So the first couple of days of the dailies were basically ignored by me. But, since we had our editor on set working every day, a few days into shooting I began getting rough cuts of entire scenes. Those gave me an incredible amount of joy because the success of filmed storytelling depends on how the footage cuts together, and I could already see we were creating story that had emotional weight; even in raw form, the edits had a feel, a tone, a tension. I could see that there was a movie here and that created this relief because it was going to work. It might not be perfect, but it was going to work.

What advice would you give a new filmmaker getting ready to tackle their first project?

Give the writing full attention. My script got in front of people because there was a famous actor behind it who told people, "This is good, you need to read it." That's rare and it's lucky, but I partially made my own luck by writing the hell out of the screenplay. The truth of the matter is, what got the film made was that people started to read the script and wanted to turn the page to see what happened next. Without a doubt, the screenplay is the most critical part of the process. So even though film is a visual medium, I would say to anyone, you need to read your script as if you don't know what is going to happen. You have to hear the lines in your head as if a person is actually going to say them believably, and you have to be very tough on your writing. That, to me, is your best chance at making your film stand out without spending a dime. If the script is good enough, the process of making the movie and gluing it all together can be very forgiving. Because if the spine of the story is in there, if it says something meaningful, then the actors and department heads have a map they can hold onto. You're all rowing in the same direction, and what comes out the other side is more likely to be a cohesive piece of art than just an assembly of scenes. ◆

Charlie Tyrell

MY DEAD DAD'S PORNO TAPES (2018) | DOCUMENTARY

Synopsis: A short documentary that follows director Charlie Tyrell as he tries to uncover a better understanding of his deceased father through the random objects he inherited, including a pile of dirty VHS movies.

Was there a specific time in your life when you realized that you wanted to be a filmmaker?

When I was younger I had an aptitude for visual arts in a general sort of way. Filmmaking wasn't something that was that accessible to me; we didn't have a family camcorder that I could go play around with. It wasn't until I enrolled in a university film program that it became something that I could explore.

Did you go to school for film or video production, and was it what you expected it to be?

I went to Ryerson University which is now Toronto Metropolitan University. I got a bachelor of fine arts in film studies, so I had a good mix of practical as well as theoretical knowledge. I was doing film productions while I was learning about film theory. It was such an unknown for me that I didn't know what to expect, but I followed my impulses to go there and I'm grateful that I did.

What attracted you to the topic of *My Dead Dad's Porno Tapes?*

When you lose someone in your life it's extremely difficult to process. As time goes by there are less and less opportunities to speak about them, keep them alive and remember them. As those opportunities dwindled a bit I receded to my dad's objects because it was a space where I could think about him, remember him and reflect on him. That's how this whole process started. It was my own way of grieving him and through that experience I began to consider it as a creative exploration through a film.

Before you shot a single scene, what were the first things you did to get up and running?

The very first thing was talking about the project with my collaborators, and I basically said, "Hey, I have this idea but I'm not sure it's a film," and I listened to their feedback. That was my starting point, and when they responded positively, it gave me the encouragement to pursue the next steps.

Did you have a budget? Did you do any fundraising?

My Dead Dad's Porno Tapes was financed with a grant from bravoFACTUAL. They had an open call where you could submit, and we wound up submitting twice before we became successful and got the grant.

What was the biggest unforeseen problem?

It was very interesting to take something like personal grief and turn it into a job that required that filmic balance of professionalism and creativity. It was a welcome challenge. However, there was the emotional weight of it; to be making a personal film and having the vulnerability to open up wasn't something I had done before. That was the biggest challenge, and not that it was unforeseen, but no matter how much you might anticipate something like that, there is still a strange way that those emotions sneak up on you.

How long did the project take you and was it longer or shorter than you expected?

It's difficult to say. It took us a couple of years to develop a budget and find a grant that would support us. Before that I sat with the idea for a few years to see if I really wanted to pursue it. So there was a lot of prep work that's difficult to account for or put onto a timeline. However, from when we got our grant to the final finished product, it was roughly 6-8 months.

How many film festivals did you submit to and how many did you get into?

Sundance was our first festival. When you play at a festival like Sundance, other festival programmers are there, and they will invite you to their festivals. We wound up not submitting to as many festivals because we got invited to quite a few. It was somewhere around 50 festivals that we played.

What did you learn from the film festival process?

Affirming their importance. Film festivals are where I've gotten jobs, where I've made connections and where I've found other people to collaborate with.

What was your most memorable or enjoyable moment during this process?

There are professional successes from this film and there are personal successes from this film. The professional success was being able to premier at Sundance. I know Sundance is known for having really narrow odds of acceptance, but I'm not sure people understand how truly narrow it is.

On a personal level, there was a lot of emotional baggage that I had with my dad. This film felt like a way to relieve myself of that burden in a way. That was something I wasn't thinking about while making the film, but it was really neat to introduce a bunch of strangers to my dad and to have them connect with him and see him for who he is, and to see him as I saw him. That accomplishment was worth more than anything else.

What advice would you give a new filmmaker getting ready to tackle their first project?

The cynical side of me, which I try to avoid, says that surviving in this medium is a war of attrition; if you stick around long enough, you will be allowed in. It's really difficult to find your people. However, despite all that, if you are so possessed to pursue this, there are those moments that things just happen, and things just connect in a way that you wouldn't believe. Those moments — which are sometimes so sparse — make it all worth it. Those times make you forget about the agony and depression you have experienced. It is one of the greatest challenges but it has the greatest rewards as well. It is a very difficult community to figure out how to be a part of, but when you do find your people, you'll discover there's always room for another good filmmaker. ◆

Cody Blue Snider

FOOL'S DAY (2013) | COMEDY

Synopsis: Fool's Day is a comedy about a 4th grade class that pulls an innocent, April Fool's Day prank on their teacher ... that accidentally kills her. Convinced they will all go to prison; the blood-covered kids try to cover up the murder and dispose of the body before their D.A.R.E officer shows up for his weekly lesson.

Was there a specific time in your life when you realized that you wanted to be a filmmaker?

Yes. I always loved movies. When you're younger, you identify with the actors first, so I wanted to be an actor. Then as I got older and a little more mature, I would get moved by a motion picture. I was like, "Who wrote that? I want to be a writer." At that point I didn't realize what a director did, but then I began taking video production classes. I was probably around 15 years old, and growing up in a family with a famous father, I always wanted to find that thing that I was best at. I remember throwing together a project for my first video production class; the teacher played it and nobody else would show theirs after mine. That was the first time that I had done something effortlessly, without trying, and I was the best at it. And that's where I realized that this is my thing. Everything else prior had been an uphill battle, but this seemed natural to me. I decided then that this is what I was going to focus on.

Did you go to school for film or video production, and was it what you expected it to be?

I went to film school on a partial scholarship using a trailer from a high school film I made called *Lakota*. I went to the School of Visual Arts in Manhattan. I did a semester and then I got an opportunity to become a director's assistant for Adam Green on a horror movie called *Frozen*. Once I had that opportunity, I dropped out of film school to work on it. A lot of my favorite filmmakers didn't go to film school or dropped out of film school. My parents are both college dropouts, so I think I had it in my head that I was going to drop out of school.

What attracted you to the topic of *Fool's Day*?

I had never seen anything like it before. For *Fool's Day*, I applied mathematical structure to it, I formulaically put it in a feature structure and collapsed it to 15-20 minutes so that it played like a feature. The idea when this came about was, okay this has two opposite polarities, it has innocence and it has murder, so I could build a style from that. I also considered that I could keep it self-contained, because it all took place in a school. And at the end of the day, it made me laugh.

Before you shot a single scene, what were the first things you did to get up and running?

First comes the idea. My brother had this idea of kids accidentally killing someone. So I loved that idea and I had wanted for a long time to make a movie all shot from the eye level of a child. I took that idea and built everything out from there.

Did you have a budget? Did you do any fundraising?

The messed up thing about being a filmmaker is it costs money. My parents had an account for my college education set up, but since I had dropped out, they said I could use some of it to make this movie. It wasn't enough to make the entire film, but it was at least a start. Then from there we went to Kickstarter. The whole thing was Kickstarter, friends and family.

What was the biggest unforeseen problem?

The first thing that happened was the lens fell off the truck and cracked. We shot on a busted lens the entire time. I'm not sure how to answer this, the whole thing was a problem. My adage is your movie is made in pre-production, destroyed in production and salvaged in post. From day one we immediately fell behind. That's what happens. There's never enough time and there's always problems. It's filmmaking, its chaos.

How long did the project take you and was it longer or shorter than you expected?

It took two years from concept to premiere at Tribeca, and there was no way I thought it would take that long.

How many film festivals did you submit to and how many did you get into?

I submitted an uncolored, unmixed and no visual effects version to Sundance because I was going to miss the deadline, but it didn't wind up getting in. *Fool's Day* wound up playing at more than 100 film festivals and won close to 50 awards including three Oscar-qualifying film festivals.

What did you learn from the film festival process?

When I finished the film, I submitted it to Tribeca. Two weeks later I got a call from them asking me if anyone has seen this or does anyone have this? I told them no and they asked if I would give it to them to premiere it. That's when I realized that when you make something good, the world opens up for you. It has played at Cannes and a ton of other big festivals, and I never submitted to any festival after Tribeca.

What was your most memorable or enjoyable moment during this process?

I think the most memorable moment was playing the movie at Tribeca, and watching the audience's faces when the head explodes. Writing the movie with my brother was the most enjoyable thing. Also, just making it with my family, and I had never done something that was so well received at the time.

What advice would you give a new filmmaker getting ready to tackle their first project?

Every story is about someone who wants something, takes action to achieve it, comes into conflict and ultimately changes. If you have those things, you have a good story. The shorter the better; do something unique and different. Try to make something self-contained to keep the budget down. This will ultimately become your calling card; what people know you by. Make something that will surprise people and is interesting. ◆

James Khanlarian

THE GHOST TRAP (2024) | DRAMA

Synopsis: The haunting story of Jamie Eugley, a young lobsterman struggling with the grinding responsibilities of a head-injured fiancé and mounting trap wars in a small Maine lobstering community.

Was there a specific time in your life when you realized that you wanted to be a filmmaker?

No, I wanted to be a lot of different things long before I wanted to be a filmmaker. In particular, I wanted to be a comic book artist. Ever since I was little, I would go around and replicate the Marvel Comics *X-Men* and *Spiderman*. At the same time, I was always writing stories, especially comedies. And on top of that I was a math scholar; I wound up going to college as a math major. None of those things that were interesting to me at the time had to do with film. But if you combine them, it becomes film. It's almost like Richard Wagner's concept where he says it's a "synthesis of arts." There's a German term for this synthesis of the arts called "Gesamthkunstwerk." It means a synthesis of all of the arts: visual arts, music, dance, language and story. Richard Wagner, who was around before film, used this synthesis for opera, particularly his ring cycle. If Wagner were alive today, he would easily be the greatest director and he would use that synthesis in film. It's the same concept for me. If you take comic book art, writing and math skills, those combined become film. Nothing else balances those skills. Film wound up applying to all my strengths, so you could say it wound up choosing me.

Did you go to school for film or video production, and was it what you expected it to be?

I did go to school for media production, but it was not the first thing I went to school for. I first went to school for math, and I was fully intending to be a mathematician, maybe a math professor and then focus on theoretical mathematics as a scholarly endeavor. I wound up getting very bored of that, very quickly.

For some reason everyone had always encouraged me to act, so I thought I would give theatre a try. I realized that I wasn't a very good actor, but I learned about acting and directing through theatre. That was a big influence on some of my desires to make movies. I transferred schools and majored in communications, which is a cheap imitation of a film program, but they taught us video production and covered some film theory. Unfortunately, they just don't teach you what it takes to make a movie. They'll tell you about focus and depth of field, they'll tell you *Citizen Kane* was great for this reason, they'll tell you *Casablanca* was the greatest film ever written and they'll teach you the three-act structure, but they don't tell you at all what it takes to make a movie.

So yes, I did go to school for media production, but I would not recommend it to anyone.

What attracted you to the topic of *The Ghost Trap*?

My business partner stumbled upon the book thinking it was a horror book. He read it and loved it and he said, "James, we need to get the rights to this." We optioned it without me even reading the book. Then I read it, and it was really good. It's a very heartfelt everyman character. The topics of the book are very comfortable, and it feels like something anybody could go through. The setting of lobster fishing in Maine is something that feels like something I could have grown up doing — working with your hands, out there on the water every day. There was a point after high school where I thought maybe I could move to the Outer Banks and work on a shrimp boat for a year before college. I never did that, so I'm glad I did this film instead. It was a very familiar topic and something I could relate to. The protagonist was carrying the weight of the world on his shoulders and I felt that when I read it. It was very real.

Before you shot a single scene, what were the first things you did to get up and running?

One of the biggest hurdles we faced when we optioned *The Ghost Trap* was Covid. We were just a small startup production company at the time, so

Covid hit us hard. It was almost two years of us treading water. We had the author of the book do the first draft of the screenplay, which really helped. After Covid started going away we immediately focused on casting.

Casting is the biggest thing, because if you don't get the right cast, no matter how beautifully a movie is shot, the wrong cast will ruin it. I previously knew Zak Steiner and had tested him for a different movie that wasn't produced. He's an actor on the verge of stardom who hasn't had this type of meaty role because he's so good looking that he gets typecast all the time. It started with Zak and then it all came together. When you have the right leading man that goes really far.

I spoke to Zak's manager who was representing Steven Ogg at the time, and once I got Steven, the project became legitimate. Steven isn't necessarily a household name, but he's known within the industry and respected among his peers. We then wound up getting Xander Barkley and Sarah Clarke. So here I am, an unknown director, with an unknown cinematographer and I had a quality cast. That helped make the project happen.

Did you have a budget? Did you do any fundraising?

We had a production budget initially of $600,000.00, and that was based on pre-Covid numbers. Then we got to Maine and realized we needed to bring our crew in from out of state because Maine doesn't have a lot of crew, so we had additional hotel expenses, etc. Our final budget wound up being $1.2M, so we doubled what we initially planned. That sounds bad but it really wasn't, because that $1.2M included post costs as well. My investors were okay with the additional money needed because they were happy with the results they were seeing and they believed in the story.

What was the biggest unforeseen problem?

One of the biggest problems I didn't expect was how difficult it was filming with boats. Everybody told me it was going to be difficult; I just wasn't aware of how tricky it was going to be. Filming with the boats slowed everything down. Every shoot has its troubles, but for the most part, our film went really well.

How long did the project take you and was it longer or shorter than you expected?

You buy film rights to a property without expectations that it will be made — its more hope that it will get made. There are too many projects that wind up falling apart. So, there was no expected timeline to get it made. It's been four years since we got the rights, and Covid was in the middle of it, and that cost us two years. But now it's been about a year and a half since we filmed, and the film has been done for several months already; we are just waiting for the right time to release it. As far as expectations are concerned, it happened much faster than expected in some sense. We filmed it in a very timely manner and post went by much more quickly than any film I've ever worked on.

How many film festivals did you submit to and how many did you get into?

We have submitted to 16 and have been accepted into one, and we were a semi-finalist in another one. We were aiming for the top film festivals, so it doesn't hurt that bad, but I also think politics are against us right now.

What did you learn from the film festival process?

I'm still learning the film festival process. It's very confusing to me because I've been told a lot of different things. I expected other people to be experts at this, and the experts are telling me things that don't quite add up. What I've learned is that film festivals are very political, and they all have their own agenda they want to push. I believe we have a very nice film on our hands, so it's very disheartening. I'm still learning the process.

What was your most memorable or enjoyable moment during this process?

It's all blurred together as one event for me. I just remember being there on set with a great cast and crew and making magic happen. I remember one night hanging out with the cast while having a few drinks and just laughing and having a good time. Hanging out with the lobstermen was memorable and all the people who helped us. I went lobster fishing for the first time which was amazing. One of the greatest moments when we were filming — there is a moment when our lead actor Zak does this long walk down a hallway, his character is completely broken at this point, this is his breakdown, and it's such an emotional scene. As we were filming we all felt it, I think half the crew was crying. The first take seemed perfect, but I knew he had another better one in him, so we did a second take, and everybody cried again.

What advice would you give a new filmmaker getting ready to tackle their first project?

The best advice is to persevere and never give up, set a goal and no matter what anybody says, be confident in your decisions and keep at it. You're constantly going to have people second-guessing you. You have to be the driving force and you have to do it your way. You have to do it and never give up. You have to find a way to get it done. A director has to be a problem solver. ◆

Tyler MacIntyre

TRAGEDY GIRLS (2017) | HORROR

Synopsis: This film follows two death-obsessed girls who use their online show about real-life tragedies to send their small town into a frenzy, and wind up becoming modern horror legends.

Was there a specific time in your life when you realized that you wanted to be a filmmaker?

For me it was probably when I was in high school. No one in my family worked in entertainment, but I was very interested and attracted to movies early on. I used to draw a lot when I was younger and then I started playing around with still cameras and video cameras, and making little projects here and there, and I wound up getting more organized in high school. I remember there was a teachers' strike for about six weeks, and my best friend and I decided we were going to make as elaborate a film as we could with all the kids we knew since there was no school. We shot an action comedy on my Hi8 camera and edited it on an old iMac. It was way too long at like 35 minutes, but it was very fun and once it was done I received a lot of positive feedback from family and friends, which helped me start to realize that I wanted to make movies for a living. It took me a lot longer to admit to myself that it was a viable career, but it all started in high school making movies with friends.

Did you go to school for film or video production, and was it what you expected it to be?

I did go to film school, but I went for graduate school. I studied psychology first in college, but was making films pretty seriously during my spare time, so I had been at it for five or six years when I started. It's very much a system of you get out what you put into it. I grew up in a small town with about 5,000 people and there was no film industry there at all. I didn't know anyone who made movies, so I was self-taught early on. A lot of my learning was trial and error, watching DVD commentary about filmmaking and reading books like *Rebel Without a Crew* by Robert Rodriguez. When I was getting my psychology degree, I probably made about 50 short films. Everybody at the time was thinking, "oh this is the guy with the film hobby, he is eventually going to settle down and become a psychologist," but I was thinking in my head about how do I take this to the next level? That's when I decided to go to film school for graduate school; I wanted to surround myself with like-minded film people. I wound up going to the American Film Institute in Los Angeles and did a Master of Fine Arts in film production with specialization in film editing. I thought at the time that if I didn't make it as a director, I could possibly find a post-production house and find a job as an in-house editor. I loved the AFI program, it was production-focused and you're making movies all the time. It was a better experience than what I expected it to be, but I also took charge of it because I was a little older at that point and appreciated it a bit more than if I'd gone straight away.

What attracted you to the topic of *Tragedy Girls*?

Slasher films are my favorite sub-genre of horror. The way I got into *Tragedy Girls* was a filmmaker friend of mine – Tom Morris – had seen an earlier cut of my previous film Patchwork and asked that I read the first draft of *Tragedy Girls*, which a producer he was working for, Kerry Rhodes, had optioned for a rewrite. I loved the title and the idea of making a modern slasher movie. There was enough interest to develop it, but the consensus was that it fell along the same lines as the post-*Scream* run in the late 90s/early 2000s slashers, and it wasn't breaking new ground. I was attracted to the challenge of essentially making a more modern version out of an out-of-fashion subgenre. I had a lot of trust from the producers to make it my own. This was around 2015 and at the time no one was really making slasher movies. My writing partner and I pitched the producers an entirely new concept that our central characters are the killers.

Before you shot a single scene, what were the first things you did to get up and running?

I did a lot of pre-production work because I am a bit of a planner. One of the first things I do is pull a lot of references like photos, artwork and scenes from other movies – basically anything that has the right vibe. I tend to spend a lot of time with my cinematographer, editor and production designer talking with them and getting them into the tone. We pull together those references for their individual teams. I do a lot of test shooting beforehand in an effort to make production go as smoothly as possible. I always make a detailed shot list and try to stick to that as best we can. I don't really rely on storyboarding, but I do use them sometimes for more complicated sequences to help make everyone on set feel more comfortable, particularly stunts and effects.

Did you have a budget? Did you do any fundraising?

We were lucky that we did have a small budget and we filmed in Kentucky to give the film the mid-western feel but to also take advantage of their new film incentive program. I had to do some minor fundraising late in the process, but the producers did a really great job sheltering me from having to worry about that, they let me stay focused on the creative side. Often, directors have to wear both hats, which I've done many times before, but for this film, I didn't really have to worry about that side of the production too much.

What was the biggest unforeseen problem?

We didn't have one disaster that springs to mind. Going in we knew that the schedule was going to be tight. We had more locations, actors, stunts and effects than you would normally want to have with our budget and timeline. The biggest unforeseen problem for me was fatigue. The lesson that I really got out of this one was that full feature films need to be treated like a marathon. Horror films usually shoot a lot at night, and I saw that this one really ran people down, and it's difficult to get people to do their best work when they're exhausted after a long string of all-night shoots. There were several times on set that things got very tense, but everybody rallied and we were able to get it done. I learned a lot about how to determine people's energy levels and get out in front of it as best as I can.

How long did the project take you and was it longer or shorter than you expected?

The whole process was a little faster than what I have come to expect. It was right around a year from our first meeting about the script to when we are on set shooting. That was a quick timeline since we wrote multiple drafts, had to get actors attached and all the financing in place. The production itself was only 22 days which is probably less than average considering all the different locations we had. We started writing it in summer 2015, shot it during summer 2016, premiered it in spring 2017 and it came out in the fall of 2017. I would say the whole process was slightly quicker than normal.

How many film festivals did you submit to and how many did you get in?

The producers sent a work in progress to the programmers of a few festivals in the fall as we were editing it. When you are submitting a movie in the fall, you're usually looking at Sundance, SXSW, Tribeca and TIFF in chronological order for your premiere the next year. Tribeca invited us to premiere first and then a day later SXSW invited us. Sundance sent us some nice feedback but passed as did TIFF. SXSW was where we thought our best fit was and we were happy to have our premiere there because it's a fun festival. Since we got that big premiere at a well-known festival, we got a lot of press and wound up getting invited to many more film festivals. I'm not sure how many we applied to, but I personally went to over a dozen festivals promoting the film.

What did you learn from the film festival process?

I think one of the biggest misconceptions with film festivals is that it's a level playing field. Film festivals are a business. Many selections, especially features, are invited, or sent directly to the festival programmer. They aren't coming through the regular submission channels like FilmFreeway. The chances of an at-large submission getting accepted to a major festival is much lower than a referred submission. I suggest that you find champions for your film early on, because that is only going to help you with the film festival process. These are ideally other festival programmers but can also be other filmmakers that are alumni of the festival you're targeting, or sales agents if you're working on a feature.

What was the most memorable or enjoyable moment during this whole process?

My favorite moments are often that first day, when you see the actors playing the characters that we've been talking about for so long. There's something magical about seeing it all come together. I really enjoyed shooting on location. We were in a small town in Kentucky, everyone was out there for weeks on end, we were stuck there together and we all became very close. I've stayed close to a lot of them, and its fun seeing their next projects, and watching them go off and expand their careers.

What advice would you give a new filmmaker getting ready to tackle their first project?

I would encourage you to find people you can climb the ladder with. I think a lot of people don't want to work on a movie if they are not creatively in charge of it, and I think that is the wrong way to look at it. I spent years crewing on other people's films and that helped me when I wanted to start making my own films. People who you work hard for will work hard for you. I think finding a group of people who can all help each other with their products is the best way to cut through the noise. Work for people who need help making their projects, because when you need help, they will be there for you. ◆

Destiny Soria

CHRISTMAS SLASHER (2024) | HORROR

Synopsis: As the holiday season rolls in, Slasher, a murderous zombie reindeer, wreaks havoc on the small town of Vixen, Minnesota.

Was there a specific time in your life when you realized that you wanted to be a filmmaker?

It all started when I was auditioning for film roles, and I wasn't landing them. I decided that I wanted to do my own films. At the time I wasn't noticing a lot of films that had female empowerment roles, so I decided to take that on.

Did you go to school for film or video production, and was it what you expected it to be?

I went to school for acting and modeling and I wound up learning filmmaking through YouTube and being on set.

What attracted you to the topic of *Christmas Slasher*?

When I was a child, my mother would take me to the theatre. We saw films like *Beetlejuice* and *A Nightmare on Elm Street* because she was into horror. I wound up falling in love with the genre. I had never seen any movies that involved reindeers killing anyone, so I decided that I wanted to try something new.

Before you shot a single scene, what were the first things you did to get up and running?

I began doing some research, basically looking at other filmmakers and learning how they used crowdfunding to finance their films. I reached out to a few of them who were successful and talked to them about the process. I wound up using Indiegogo to raise money for a short film which then led to this feature.

Did you have a budget? Did you do any fundraising?

Christmas Slasher – which is coming out later this year – was crowdfunded on Indiegogo. It did very well but I ran into a lot of questionable people, and it became very stressful. Robert Rodriguez did clinical studies to raise money for his films in the beginning, so that's what I did to raise extra money.

What was the biggest unforeseen problem?

I had so many problems I can't name them all. This was my first feature film. I am a compassionate and caring person, but I realized that sometimes people you think you can trust aren't necessarily looking out for your best interests. My kindness on this film got used by people who did not care about this creative process. I also wound up losing a couple of editors on the project, so it was delayed a few times. I am a very spiritual person, so I like to cleanse myself of the negativity and move forward.

How long did the project take you and was it longer or shorter than you expected?

The idea for my full feature was in 2016, but actually getting to work on it was 2019. I wound up doing a short film, which turned out to be really good, and I took that short film and wrote a script around it, turning it into a feature during COVID. With it coming out in 2024, it will be eight years since my original idea.

How many film festivals did you submit to and how many did you get in?

I have not submitted the actual feature to any festivals yet, but I have submitted the trailer and it has won a few awards. The trailer has led to a few film festivals expressing interest in showing the film when its complete, so I'm very blessed about that.

What did you learn from the film festival process?

From my experiences with previous shorts, I like to do my research to make sure the film festival I'm entering is right for my film. Sometimes the communication isn't great, but overall I've had good experiences.

What was the most memorable or enjoyable moment during this whole process?

There was a scene that involved a playground with kids. They were in a scene where they get killed and they were having such a great time with it. They made my day by having fun and being silly.

What advice would you give a new filmmaker getting ready to tackle their first project?

I would say to just keep going. No matter how hard the struggle is, whatever failures you run into, just keep going. Its blood, sweat and tears working as a horror filmmaker. You just have to keep going. ◆

Festivals

PART 2

As I began interviewing directors for this book, I realized that I should look into film festivals also. What are film festivals? Where are they? How do they work? Is my film good enough to submit?

Almost every director's goal is to get mass distribution for their film. Get it in front of people, lots of people. For big budget Hollywood films, distribution is not an issue. There's a term in Hollywood referred to as the "big five." If you're making a film for one of these studios, chances are the masses are going to see it. But what about the rest of us? How can we get our movie seen?

That's where independent film festivals come in. These festivals are held at smaller venues around the country. Some festivals specialize in a certain genre like horror or documentary filmmaking. These venues are where rising filmmakers can show their films to smaller crowds, and build a name for themselves.

Once I completed my first short documentary I entered the film festival process. I went online and started looking at festivals around my area and state. I submitted to festivals just to apply. I figured if I submitted to as many as I could, the chances of my film getting selected went up. However, that wasn't the case. Also, it can be expensive entering all of those festivals; if each one has a fee, that adds up quickly. Out of more than 20 submissions, my film got accepted to two and screened at one festival. I was super excited about that one screening, I had finally made it. But I was still unsure of how they worked. Why did mine get selected here and nowhere else? Who was watching these films?

While I was working on this book in 2019 I was asked to be a judge for The West Chester Film Festival in West Chester, PA. I had volunteered there for a few years, just working the door and taking tickets over one weekend while the festival went on. That year, however, one of the volunteers asked me if I wanted to do more, and by more, she meant being on a panel and selecting the films that would win at the festival. The films had already been screened, now they just wanted to pick winners for each category. I jumped at the opportunity.

One Saturday in April I met at an organizer's house at 8:00 in the morning and watched short films until 4:30 in the afternoon. It was a long and interesting day. I was on a panel of three and after each film we would discuss what we liked and didn't like. It was three films per genre. We sat in that living room all day and discussed these films. It was awesome. I learned a lot. One of the most important things I learned was there are a lot of good filmmakers out there. There are also a lot of bad ones, or should I say inexperienced ones. Filmmakers who are rushing to get their movie out the door before they are actually done making it. Sound, editing and white balance issues were a few of the recurring issues I saw throughout the day.

That day gave me a lot of insight on what I had done wrong with my film, how I could have done things differently and what to do on all of my future films. It was quite the learning experience and I really enjoyed it.

In this section, I interviewed all different types of people who are involved in film festivals. I wanted to get their side of the process, see what they had to say about independent filmmaking and what they hope will continue to happen in the future of filmmaking.

Reading Film Festival

DR. CHRIS WOODWARD
ASSOCIATE DIRECTOR — JUROR COORDINATOR

What got you interested in independent filmmaking?

I always found that some small budget films really pop out and you say to yourself, "This is absolutely incredible." These small films may cost upward of a million dollars, while Hollywood movies cost tens or hundreds of millions, and this small film is just amazing. Getting to see what people can do with limited funds is extremely interesting and being able to discover these independent films has been a joy for me for many years.

What is your role at the *Reading Film Festival*?

I've been working with the Reading Film Festival since 2016. I was initially a juror, last year [2018] I was juror manager and moderator manager so I made sure all the films and film blocks had similar topics which helps the flow of the festival. I'm also involved with calling every filmmaker that is selected for the festival. In September and October, its working on getting everything set up. During the festival itself I'm running around to the different film blocks making sure the moderators are there and everything is running smoothly.

How long have you been in this role and have you had experiences similar to this in the past?

This is the first time I've been involved in a film festival.

What is the goal of *The Reading Film Festival*?

We want to be the filmmaker's film festival. I was not aware that that wasn't the way all film festivals ran. The filmmakers have expressed to us how happy and surprised they were with the overall film festival. We provide a hotel room for two nights, parties and excellent communication throughout the whole festival. They've told us that they are not used to that level of service from other festivals. For me, that's the important part. That's the thing that makes a film festival great; to have great films and have excited filmmakers who want to interact. That's been really rewarding to me.

How long does it take to get the festival up and running from start to finish?

We meet after each festival to go over some of the things we need to fix. We also have to pick our upcoming year's dates, talk about hotels and transportation. We have excellent cooperation with an IMAX theatre in Reading and another building next door called GoggleWorks which lets us use their theatre, so the venues are pretty much set, and we don't have to worry about that as much. Two months later I start contacting the jurors who have worked the previous festival and try getting commitments from them. I also begin looking into getting additional volunteers. We then open up early bird submissions. During this time, I encourage the jurors to get the films they've been assigned rated as quickly as possible, because we wind up getting a ton of submissions right before the deadline. Jurors are also asked to submit recommendations for various categories … best director, best actor, best actress and so on. There is very little downtime from when the festival ends to getting ready for the next festival.

Do you have a general budget for *The Reading Film Festival*?

I really don't know those figures. We have a lot of donations and transportation and hotels work with us on discounts. I know that we break even, however if we continue to grow the way we've been growing at some point we may need a full-time person on staff.

On average how many film submissions do you receive each year?

Two years ago in 2017 it was 85; last year it was 121 and in 2019 we are expecting 150+. I've ramped up the number of jurors to make sure we have the proper manpower to rate all of these films. So the festival continues to grow each year. FilmFreeway, which lists about 7,000 film festivals around the world, has been listing our festival in the top 100 based on filmmaker feedback. I'm naive about this but I want this to be the Sundance of the East. Some people would look at me and think I'm crazy, but I don't know why we can't do it.

Out of those submissions, how many are watching them and considering them for the festival?

Our goal is three reviewers per film. Last year out of 121, I believe 48 were selected. That's all durations too, shorts and a few features. We stay pretty close to 50 because there is only a certain amount of time that we can allot to film blocks.

What advice do you have for a filmmaker who is getting ready to tackle their first film?

When you submit to a film festival you want to make sure you complete everything they are asking for. Make sure they look at the festival, review previous films, make sure it's a fit for the film they're planning on submitting. In terms of the creative process I think a lot of the filmmakers who submit are getting feedback from family and friends and people that they worked with on the film. I think it may be useful to screen it with people they don't know so they can get a more accurate appraisal of the film. It's often difficult for family or friends to tell a filmmaker, maybe you need to cut this scene, or this should be changed around. And finally pick your film festival wisely. Look at what people have said about it. Don't just pick it because its close. ◆

Scares That Care Film Festival

MICHAEL LOMBARDO | FESTIVAL DIRECTOR

What got you interested in independent filmmaking?

I've always been a horror film fanatic. I grew up as a video store kid, so I would roam the aisles looking for weirdo horror films based on the cool cover art on the VHS boxes. I got really into movies like *Evil Dead*, and Peter Jackson's early work like *Dead Alive*. I watched a lot shot on video as a kid and it kind of inspired me to try it myself. My goal was to always become a filmmaker. *Evil Dead* was made with a group of friends who had just gotten out of college and I was like, "I can do that." I started teaching myself special effects and filmmaking and I've been doing it since I was a kid. Fifteen years later, I have a full feature under my belt, won a bunch of awards, made a lot of shorts and now I run a couple of film festivals. It's all been a pretty wild ride.

What is your role at *The Scares That Care Film Festival*?

The Scares That Care is a horror-themed children's charity that runs year round and once a year we have a convention called The Scares That Care Charity Weekend. This is my second year running the festival.

How long have you been in this role and have you had experiences similar to this in the past?

This is my second season running The Scares That Care but I've also been running the Horror Night of the Lancaster International Short Film Festival for the last five years. I'm also a judge for the Pennsylvania Indie Short Film Festival and The GenreBlast Film Festival.

What is the goal of *The Scares That Care Film Festival*?

It is to help families in need especially with children. We do that by running these events with the horror community. Kane Hodder is a member of the board and Sid Haig from all of the Rob Zombie films was a big donor. All of these people come and support the charity and they donate money and do auctions for signed memorabilia and 100% of that goes to these families and children in need. Everyone is a volunteer. Nobody gets paid.

How long does it take to get the festival up and running from start to finish?

Once we know that there will be another event and the dates are set, then we create a call for entries. There's a whole bunch of different deadlines with different price points. After that final date, we are then responsible for taking all of those shorts and judging everything and figuring out what we want to play. This whole process will ideally be done three months before the festival because we want to give the filmmakers as much notice as possible to set up travel arrangements. It's a year-round process.

Do you have a general budget for *The Scares That Care Film Festival*?

I am not involved in the financial end of the festival, that's all part of the convention. As far as other festivals go, I don't have exact numbers, but I know it's very expensive to hold a film festival. Submission fees and ticket sales do play a part in the overall budget. Generally, the sad truth is, film festivals are not making money. It's not a profitable thing to do despite what people think. You need a venue, you need a projection rental, sound, ticket sales, crowd control and judges. It's a lot of overhead and just not profitable.

On average how many film submissions do you receive each year?

For Scares That Care 2018 we had around 100–150. This year [2019] so far we have about 90 with several months left. When filmmakers submit and they don't get in and they get upset, they don't realize the sheer volume of movies they're competing against, and there is only so much you can program over one weekend. During the festival we are only playing 30-40% of the submissions we originally received.

Out of those submissions, how many people are watching them and considering them for the festival?

That's a completely fest-by-fest basis. Generally you want at least two judges to watch each submission. There's a lot of films that you watch and you know that they will not be contenders, but when you get down to the core group of films that are neck and neck, you want multiple eyes on them deciding which ones get in. The Scares That Care I have final say on what gets in.

What advice do you have for a filmmaker who is getting ready to tackle their first film?

My absolute number one is do not make short films over 15 minutes long. Nobody wants to hear that, but when we get a 20–25 minute short submission, I can pretty much guarantee it's not going to get picked. A short film block is generally 1 to 1 ½ hours long; when you give someone a 30-minute film, you now have to cater that block around that film. It makes it extremely difficult to program based around that film. If you put on a 10-minute short and your audience isn't into it, its fine because it's over in 10 minutes. If that same film was 30 minutes, you'll lose your audience and they'll walk out, and then everybody loses. Anything under 15 minutes is beautiful. ◆

PA Indie Shorts Film Festival

SAMANTHA KOLESNIK | FESTIVAL FOUNDER AND DIRECTOR

What got you interested in independent filmmaking?

I'm a lifelong film fan. The movies that play at the mainstream theatres are great, but they don't always interest me. I think there is a lot of really amazing and thought-provoking work out there being made by independent artists, and you don't get to see them as much as you get to see the big blockbusters.

What is your role at *The PA Indie Shorts Film Festival*?

I'm the founder and festival director so I handle all the operations of the festival.

How long have you been in this role and have you had experiences similar to this in the past?

I have been the festival director of PA Indie for the past two years and prior to that I was co-founder and co-director of The Women in Horror Film Festival in Georgia. Also during those years I served as a guest juror at Les Femmes Underground Film Festival and a screenplay judge for both Nightmares Film Festival and GenreBlast Film Festival.

What is the goal of *The PA Indie Shorts Film Festival*?

To celebrate the art of short film and to bring it to the community in northeastern Pennsylvania. Short film has a hard road in the United States, it's not as celebrated here as it is in Europe. I have a passion for it and I wanted to provide an opportunity to celebrate it as an art form.

How long does it take to get the festival up and running from start to finish?

It takes all year, mostly because it is an ongoing process. A lot of people start film festivals and get burnt out pretty quickly because they don't realize all the work involved. You have to secure a venue, funding and sponsors, develop a method for submissions and decide whether or not you are going to present awards. Then you have to assemble a team to help you solicit and screen the submissions. Reviewing and talking about the films is a huge process. Beyond that there are the onsite logistics — how are we going to get the filmmakers from point A to point B. And finally, there's drafting up press releases to make sure the films get the attention they need. Its very time consuming.

Do you have a general budget for *The PA Indie Shorts Film Festival?*

It depends on the type of festival you are running. If you are running a small community festival it could cost a few thousand dollars. If you are running a bigger festival in a major city you could be talking tens of thousands of dollars and up. It's really a sliding scale based on the location and venue you find and how big you want to make the festival.

On average how many film submissions do you receive each year?

I can't remember the exact number but it's more than 500. A few factors play into this number. One is we have very reasonable entry fees — our early entry fee is around $7.00. I'm a filmmaker too, so I know how expensive it can get submitting to film festival after film festival. I'm trying to keep it low and affordable for filmmakers. So I think we get more submissions because of that.

Out of those submissions, how many are watching them and considering them for the festival?

It was around 10 to 15 people in 2018. This year [2019], it's going to be around 30 because we're expecting more submissions.

What advice do you have for a filmmaker who is getting ready to tackle their first film?

Be strategic in your film festival run; know why you are submitting to the places you're submitting. Places where you think you can get good community support ... places that are your goal festivals ... places where you think there might be good networking. As far as the film itself, make sure its festival ready. Don't submit something that could be improved. If your sound is off, don't submit it with a cover letter stating that you're still working on the sound. Be polite — don't write the festival director asking for early decisions or for screening time switches or if you're going to win an award — things like that are completely inappropriate. Here's a good tip for our film festival; we accept 10 different genres and drama is by far the most competitive. ◆

The Cape May Film Festival

VERONICA SCUTARO | TREASURER, 2014–2017; PRESIDENT, 2017–2019

What got you interested in independent filmmaking?

I think having friends who were filmmakers, and an understanding of how hard it is for a filmmaker to see their film shown in front of a live audience. That knowledge made me sensitive to those filmmakers and my goal is to give them a platform to find an audience that they deserve.

What is your role at *The Cape May Film Festival*?

As President, I do most of the stuff that's in the background. I get venues, work with curators on creating a program and generate sponsors and advertising so we can keep it going. When the final films are selected, I am the liaison between the filmmakers and the festival.

How long have you been in this role and have you had experiences similar to this in the past?

I've been involved with the festival for five years now. I did not do this in the past. When I retired to Cape May, it was something that interested me. The folks who were involved with the festival were really interested in the arts, and they also have a teen film camp that really sparked my interest. I would say the film camp is the best part of this whole endeavor, to see kids write a script, act, edit, make their own music and then get the opportunity to show it to the public. It's a wonderful thing.

What is the goal of *The Cape May Film Festival*?

To bring film to South Jersey that the people here would not ordinarily get to see. Here, we don't have independent movie houses like they do in New York City where I'm from. There's no Film Forum, there's no Cinema Village. There's the Cape May Film Society and we want to bring the films to the people of South Jersey that they cannot see anywhere else. When people come to the festival, they're coming for the independent films and the shorts, they aren't terribly interested in commercial high-end films.

How long does it take to get the festival up and running from start to finish?

Between 10 and 11 months. One month after the festival ends the board meets and we talk about lessons learned, how we want things done for the upcoming year and what we can do to make our festival more attractive to filmmakers. Then we decide what our dates will be the following year so we can secure the venue. At about six months before the festival we begin to solicit films. At about two months out from the festival we begin to go over nitty gritty things, such as film timing and film order during the festival days. Then we host the festival.

Do you have a general budget for *The Cape May Film Festival*?

We are a nonprofit so our goal is to break even, we don't look to make money on anything. What we do get we invest into our programming and film camp.

On average how many film submissions do you receive each year?

It goes up and down. I can remember one year we got 80 films and we only had time to show 20. Last year [2018] we got 53. Depending on how long they are we have to reduce them down to 20 or less to be shown at the festival.

Out of those submissions, how many people are watching them and considering them for the festival?

There are two curators and then there are three people from the board. We all watch the films separately and when we're all done, that's when we start to pick. It's a collaborative process but our curators will generally have the last word as they are extremely experienced when it comes to film and media.

What advice do you have for a filmmaker who is getting ready to tackle their first film?

I think that people need to have the freedom to tell the story they want to tell. It's not about their plot, editing or sound. Frankly, a lot of it is about technical things behind the scenes that people don't think about. If a festival asks you to please submit both online and with a DVD, please do both of those things. Comply with the technical part of the festival because there are reasons. We are at the southern tip of New Jersey and we don't have the best connectivity. If you didn't supply a DVD originally when submitting and your film is selected and we lose service, your film will not be shown. My advice is when someone running a film festival asks you to do something that seems redundant or silly, there's usually a reason. Be assured that we want to see your work, and we wouldn't ask you to spin your wheels for no reason. Be creative and show us the story you want to tell. ◆

West Chester Film Festival

KEVIN FITZPATRICK | BOARD VICE PRESIDENT, 2017–PRESENT

What got you interested in independent filmmaking?

I have always had an interest in film. When I was at college, a lot of my friends were film majors and they of course had exposed themselves to a wider variety of films than what I had grown up with. One of the jobs I had on campus was working for the film department as the projectionist, so I was able to take classes where they were watching and analyzing movies without being a part of the film program. Through that I was able to watch a lot of fascinating old school black and white experimental independent films back when everything was an independent film. So everything from Salvador Dali to French experimental films, things that have had an influence on some major films. I can see some commercial films these days and how that played into the third man. And then The West Chester Film Festival is really where the definitive exposure came. I started watching hundreds of hours of film each year, really getting a feel for what was quality storytelling because I was watching it more critically then someone for entertainment.

What is your role at the *West Chester Film Festival*?

Currently my position is the Vice President of the Board for the West Chester Film Festival. Everyone who works for the film festival is a volunteer. We don't have any paid staff. I originally started year one as a volunteer ticket taker, usher and projectionist because I had experience with that … general fire put-er-outer. We really got lucky with the West Chester Film Festival because the way these things generally go, after somewhere around 3-5 seasons, the people that founded it tend to get burned out and quit. We got lucky because we had a depth chart, and people who were willing to step up and take those positions on the Board as people left.

How long have you been in this role and have you had experiences similar to this in the past?

This is my second year as Vice President; I spent two or three as Secretary of the Board. This is the only film festival I've been involved with.

What is the goal of The West Chester Film Festival?

The goal of the West Chester Film Festival is to bring high-quality independent films from around the world to our community. We really want to show the citizens of West Chester and Chester County the scope of what filmmakers can do and how the art of storytelling can be expressed through film. That has been the goal for about the last five or six years. Prior to that, the goal of the Board was to put a movie theatre in West Chester, but the members found that was too altruistic of a goal. So they shifted things to bringing movies in, because we enjoy seeing people's faces when they see some of these fantastic movies coming from South Korea, California or Lancaster. The types of stories that people can tell and how they impact our communities is great for us to see and something we really enjoy putting out there.

How long does it take to get the festival up and running from start to finish?

Planning is a year-round process and during each festival we are constantly coming up with new ideas that we want to implement the next year. It takes about nine months to get ready. Screening, grading, compiling, discussing, accepting, scheduling, finding venues, advertising and ordering tickets.

Do you have a general budget for *The West Chester Film Festival?*

The bulk of our budget comes from sponsorships. The secondary revenue stream is ticket sales. The filmmaker submissions balance out the cost to accept films, because the third-party film submission platform charges a fee. We try really hard to keep that balance, because we don't want to raise our submission fees to be exclusionary in any way; we want to make sure we are getting as broad a scope of films submitted as possible. We've raised our entry fees twice in 16 years and every time the subject comes up it's an argument because we want to keep the fees low.

On average how many film submissions do you receive each year?

On average about 165; in 2019 we had 172. We have a category called the Young Filmmakers category, where the filmmakers are under the age of 18 and there are no submission fees. We do get a lot of submissions through that category, but they are not calculated in the total. If I did add those, we would be in the 200–225 range.

Out of those submissions, how many are watching them and considering them for the festival?

We like to have 10. We accept a number of films that goes up to about 714 minutes. So we do our grading and then we rank everything. So if all of those films are 30 minutes long, we accept fewer films, if they are all three minutes long, we accept more. People always ask "how many films do you let in?" It all depends on how long they are, but around 60. After they are chosen, the top three of each genre go to the judges for picking the best.

What advice do you have for a filmmaker who is getting ready to tackle their first film?

Make them shorter. My wife and I are screeners, and when we're done screening, we constantly say, "That film was so good; if it was five minutes shorter it would have been great." The film was 25 minutes but if had been 18 it would have been tighter and stronger and captured our attention more. Most of the criticism we have is, make it shorter. Especially for the first-time filmmaker, because they put all this time into writing and shooting it, and I get the feeling they know it doesn't work, but they leave it in because of their attachment to the project. ◆

Oil Valley Film Festival

MATT CROYLE | FOUNDER AND FESTIVAL DIRECTOR

What got you interested in independent filmmaking?

I grew up going to the movies with my dad a lot, so from a very young age I was infatuated with what can happen on the big screen. I was also a stage actor and the two interests really fit well together; the process of creating something with other people plus the longevity and lasting impact film has on us is something that has attracted me to the medium.

What is your role at the *Oil Valley Film Festival*?

I am the founder and the festival director of the Oil Valley Film Festival.

How long have you been in this role and have you had experiences similar to this in the past?

I had no previous festival experience before we launched. This is our fifth season. This year we had to go virtual because of the ongoing global COVID-19 pandemic.

What is the goal of *Oil Valley Film Festival*?

I started the festival because Oil City, Pennsylvania, is my hometown and doesn't have a lot of cultural outlets like you'd find in major cities. I wanted to bring films to the area that showed how connected we all are as humans — films from Serbia, Russia or the Middle East that are universal stories because they are human stories. From narrative to documentary, I wanted people to become more aware of that.

How long does it take to get the festival up and running from start to finish?

I'm working on the festival all year long but not in a full-time capacity. Our festival is small enough that we don't have to worry about securing outside vendors. We continue to grow every year with the amount of submissions we receive, but we haven't reached a point where we need to start incorporating outside businesses. I have two venues for the film festival that are available to me every year, the Oil City Library and the National Transit Building, which used to house the Rockefeller Standard Oil Company. They are both historical buildings, which adds to the draw for people to attend the festival. During the festival itself, I'm there for every screening. I do have a few volunteers, but I don't rely on anyone else helping setup and breakdown, it's all me.

Do you have a general budget for *Oil Valley Film Festival*?

We don't have a general budget year to year, but the submission fees we do get go into decorating and backdrops and we also give some money back to the Library and Transit Center as a thank you for keeping the dates open for us. Overall, we have a very small operating budget.

On average how many film submissions do you receive each year?

We have gotten more submissions every year over the last five years. Being a small festival it's been quite impressive, this year we have more than 250 submissions from 17 countries.

Out of those submissions, how many are watching them and considering them for the festival?

At the present time I have three other judges. I trust their judgement in quality and filmmaking knowledge to narrow things down for me. They are each assigned specific categories and they will curate those specific categories down to a certain amount of films. I will then screen them and have final say on what gets shown or not.

What advice do you have for a filmmaker who is getting ready to tackle their first film?

I've made films myself so it's weird as somebody who creates things, to judge other people's work. It's a really awkward position to be in because I know how much time, effort, blood, sweat and tears goes into making something. I have to look at these films objectively and decide if they fit with what we're trying to do and say at the film festival.

The first thing I would say is don't wait for permission from somebody else to make something; the only permission you need is from yourself. The second thing is it doesn't have to look like a big budget movie if its done well. You don't have to have the most expensive camera. Third would be to make sure the sound is considered the most important part of the production. You could have the most beautiful movie in the world, but if you can't hear it, or the sound is distracting, it's not going to work. And the fourth would be to make sure you have something to say. ◆

Chicago Underground Film Festival, CUFF

TAILA HOWE | EXECUTIVE PRODUCER

What got you interested in independent filmmaking?

My route into the film festival industry wasn't very traditional; I come from an events production background. The whole idea of DIY mentality, doing something with just the resources that you have, drew me in.

What is your role at the *CUFF*?

I am the executive producer of the Chicago Underground Film Festival.

How long have you been in this role and have you had experiences similar to this in the past?

I've been in this role for a little over one year and I've had no experience being a film festival producer prior to CUFF.

What is the goal of *CUFF*?

CUFF is officially the longest running underground film festival in the world. The reason why it's been going on for so long and attracted such a core group of followers or cinephiles is because CUFF does not conform. We present work that more traditional film festivals would turn away. The films we screen are what we think is really cool, films that push the boundaries of traditional filmmaking and storytelling. We have close relationships with different underground movements and scenes within the city related to music, photography and filmmaking. And being in a city that has so many different societies and cultures really close to one another, CUFF is able to highlight these and show them at the festival. We stand for showing work that continues to push the boundaries of what is considered filmmaking.

How long does it take to get the festival up and running from start to finish?

About nine months. For about three to four months we have films coming in. As those films come in, they are filtered to the screening team. Once they're screened and the films are chosen, the master list gets sent to me and the other programmers. Once I see that master list, I begin to think about different brands, organizations and groups in Chicago. My job is to figure out how we can tap into different communities to figure out who would best benefit from seeing this film and why, and then that relates to different sponsors who are trying to reach that specific customer base.

Do you have a general budget for *CUFF*?

CUFF has in the past survived off of filmmaker submission fees. We have had pre-existing sponsors. Usually the festival is floated heavily by the filmmaker submission fees; that is not the way we are pivoting but it is the way the festival has skirted by.

On average how many film submissions do you receive each year?

About 5,000.

Out of those submissions, how many are watching them and considering them for the festival?

We have between 15-25 screeners, closer to the 25 range. This year we have 15 full feature films and then we have 15 shorts programs which puts us in the range of 80-90 films.

What advice do you have for a filmmaker who is getting ready to tackle their first film?

You don't need as much as you think you need; you can do it for less. You can produce a minimal viable product, something that is way less than your ideal perfectly executed production. If you want to make a film and you have a camera that can record, you can make a movie. ◆

Fans

PART 3

Chances are, you know a film fan. Someone who is always talking about movies, or whenever they see you they ask, "See anything good lately?" You might have daily conversations at your work, like I do, where everyone is talking about a certain film either in the theatre or streaming. And for those few minutes you all discuss it like film critics; some like a particular film and others don't. Your opinions may get heated at times, but that's okay, because it's part of this creative process that allows people to experience things in a different way. Someone may give you a secondhand view of a particular film that you hated, and you then decide to give it a second chance, looking at it from a different angle.

Before I got into filmmaking I really didn't know much about independent or foreign filmmaking. I was only used to the Hollywood blockbusters that were in theatres. Once I started dating my now wife, she introduced me to The Ritz Theatre in Philadelphia, where I could experience more of these films. We saw *Run Lola Run*, *The Station Agent*, *The Blair Witch Project* and *Sideways*, to name a few. It opened up my eyes to a broader landscape.

In this section I wanted to get the fans' perspective of the films they watch. People who are not involved in filmmaking in any way. But I also didn't interview them like the rest of the people in this book. For this section, I provided a questionnaire and sent it out. I wanted them to fill it out on their own. I wanted them to really think about what they were talking about, or really explaining why they loved a particular movie. I figured by doing this, it would give them time to think of things they had forgotten about as a child, or recall a movie or actor they really enjoyed watching. I wanted to get an unbiased opinion of any film they wanted to talk about.

Note: Interviewee ages have not been adjusted.

Matt D'Innocenzo

25 YEARS OLD | HIGH SCHOOL HISTORY TEACHER

Tell me a little about yourself ... Where do you live? What did you study in college? What do you do for a career?

I grew up in the small town of Mendon, Massachusetts. I was obsessed with movies as a kid and after waffling around between a few ideas of colleges and majors, I finally decided to go to Emerson College in Boston to study Writing for Film and Television. Going to a school like Emerson was eye-opening to me; before, I had never met anyone my age who had even heard of the Coen brothers. Then, suddenly, I was surrounded by hundreds of peers who loved and knew as much about movies as me, there were even people who knew more than I did. For the first time, I was exposed to what it takes to make a film happen behind the scenes, rather than experiencing cinema just as a viewer, or experimenting with screenwriting. I found myself way in over my head trying to figure out the science behind what makes film work and the technical skills needed to shoot something on actual film. I spent two years at Emerson networking, learning more about the craft, writing and discovering myself, but decided that I couldn't really imagine myself in the high-pressure world of Hollywood where selling yourself is everything and the chances of real success can be so slim. I decided to change paths to become a teacher so that I could reach individuals with my 'message' year after year, rather than pouring my heart into a script only to see it get torn apart in the industry.

What movie(s) first inspired your love of film and why?

The first movie I ever saw in the theatre was the *The Lion King*, as a three-month old baby. I don't remember that, but I imagine "The Circle of Life" had some sort of subconscious impact on me. My obsession for movies goes back farther than I can even remember; I'm told as a toddler I was also obsessed with watching VHS' of *Mary Poppins* and *Pete's Dragon*. The first movie I remember really falling in love with as a kid was actually *Clue* — a weird movie that mostly went over my head but nevertheless entertained me. Watching Tim Curry in his manic glory made me want to become an actor when I was in 2nd grade — he made it look like no job could be as fun as acting. *Fargo* would probably be the first serious 'film' I really got into when I first saw it in middle school. I loved the way it would swing between ridiculous comedy and gritty, dark violence, often all in the same scene. It's the movie that made me want to start writing screenplays, and the first one I wrote when I was in eighth grade was a complete rip-off of *Fargo*.

What types of movies are you generally attracted to?

If it's a quality film, I'll probably like it regardless of genre, but the hardest genres for me to get into would be fantasy, Westerns and really old period pieces because they're too hard to relate to. I've never been a fan of romantic films because they can be so schmaltzy, but at the same time, I will seek out queer romance films because the romantic conflicts and challenges for queer people can be so much more raw and powerful to me. My favorite genre might have to be horror, because it's the one genre where I don't really care if the movie is actually good or not. Even bad horror movies are almost always fun to watch.

Name a few performances that have blown you away.

Of course, there's far too many to list. The first one to come to mind is Al Pacino in *Dog Day Afternoon* because he feels so human and real and he covers such a range of emotions and experiences throughout the film. Gena Rowlands in *A Woman Under the Influence* is another all-time great for me — I've only seen the film once and as much as I want to watch it again, it's one I'll have to mentally prepare myself for because her performance is so heart-wrenching. In terms of just straight up making me laugh, Nathan Lane may have given one of the funniest performances ever in *The Birdcage*. There's a handful of actresses whom I will watch in anything: Julianne Moore, Cate Blanchett, Laura Linney or Toni Collette could all read a phone book and still have me entranced. I'd also have to mention pretty much any actor from an Ingmar Bergman film, particularly Liv Ullmann and Max von Sydow.

What director's films will you always watch?

Sometimes I surprise myself when it comes to this; after seeing *Carol*, I was blown away by Todd Haynes' direction and vowed I'd see anything he put out again, but I still haven't gotten myself to see his latest film *Wonderstruck* because the trailer just didn't appeal to me. I suppose I have to be drawn in by both the director and the story to really be sold. I'll admit that I do have to see every Tarantino film, if only because I know it will guarantee some interesting conversations with others. I'll eat up any Bergman or Bunuel film I can get my hands on. Paul Thomas Anderson is consistently reliable, and some of my other favorites include Steven Spielberg, David Lynch, Terry Gilliam, Alejandro Inarritu, Steven Soderbergh and the criminally underrated Sidney Lumet. This isn't one single director, but I will always go see movies produced by Pixar because their track record is so outstanding to me.

How much stock do you put in movie reviews?

I don't blindly agree with them, but they do tend to be the best indicator of how good a movie is going to be. It's pretty rare that I really hate a well-reviewed film, or love one that was panned. If a movie doesn't get great reviews, I'm almost definitely not going to see it in the theatre.

What film are you most embarrassed to admit that you love?

This is hard — I think I have a good reason for every movie I love. If I'm asked what my favorite movie is, I am embarrassed to admit it's probably *Schindler's List* because even though it isn't fun or pleasant at all, I think it's such an expertly crafted film that resonates so powerfully and unforgettably. Other film snobs tend to look down on Spielberg, but I'm unashamed in loving pretty much all of his mushy gold. There are some movies I love just for the nostalgia they evoke, especially movies I watched as a kid, like *Space Jam*.

Do you prefer to watch movies at home or in the theatre?

Theatre. It's so easy to get distracted watching movies at home. The theatre forces everything else out of your head and lets you escape into the world of cinema. Plus, movies are so enhanced by the reactions of a big audience.

Comedies are funnier when everyone's laughing, and horror movies are scarier when everybody gasps at once.

What aspect of film appeals to you the most: genre, dialogue, acting, cinematography or something else?

My main focus is always the writing — I love movies with powerful themes, complicated characters, rich dialogue and surprising plots. I appreciate the other elements of film on top of that, but you need a great script to make a good movie.

What advice would you give to an aspiring filmmaker?

I'd say to get as familiar as you can with all the different aspects of filmmaking. Filmmaking to me is the ultimate collaborative art; it takes so many components to make a great film. You won't be an expert in every craft, but you can't make a good movie without understanding to some extent what everyone else is contributing and how you can work with them. ◆

$\mathcal{JP}$ *(prefer to remain anonymous)*

44 YEARS OLD | CORPORATE VIDEO TEAM LEAD

Tell me a little about yourself ... Where do you live? What did you study in college? What do you do for a career?

I live in Pennsylvania and went to a big SportsBall University. It wasn't a bad school but it wasn't for me. I've only ever been to a single football game. The only thing I remember about it was me and my brothers getting in trouble for throwing marshmallows. We were either asked to leave or got bored. I don't remember. The place wasn't for me or rather, I wasn't for it. I had no idea what I wanted out of life but I thought I did. I graduated with a degree in Aerospace Engineering, mostly because I thought it sounded hard and wanted people to think I'm smart. I skipped at least one class a day — we had the Canadian channel (and Fox) in the dorms so I could get a full three episodes of *The Simpsons* in before nap and dinner. Had I gone directly into filmmaking, I would have had a shitty-ass work ethic and had no stories to tell. Twenty years later, doing what it takes to make a living for my family and sometimes affording the things I want, I've learned more about all aspects of film than any college could teach me. Or at least, I think so. Still, given a second chance, I'd major in filmmaking.

What movie(s) first inspired your love of film and why?

I'm an 80s child so anything and everything* from the late 70s and 80s inspired me. *Star Wars* was a huge one for me. The summer before third grade, we spent a lot of time in the hospital visiting my grandmother with terminal cancer. For a mid-day break up, my parents would take us to movies near the hospital. I saw *Back to the Future* three times in the theatre that summer. It is my favorite movie of all time. And it is my wife's favorite movie of all time too.

At Christmas time when I was in second grade, I remember my parents telling me and my two brothers that they had a special surprise for us. We were certain it was a VCR. We didn't have a VCR yet. Everyone had a VCR at this point. It wasn't a VCR. It was a black lab puppy. I have so many fun memories of that doggo. Sometime after that, I don't remember when, we did get a VCR.

We didn't have cable TV until I was almost done high school. But in semi-rural PA, when you do have a VCR, going to the movie rental store was just about the only thing to do. In junior high school, I would go to the movie theatre almost every single weekend and sometimes twice a weekend. It was usually to be with girls. I saw anything that we could get into.

In high school, I had a job at a movie theatre. Like most jobs I had back then, it didn't last long. But this time, it wasn't a choice of mine. After my glorious few weeks at the movie theatre, I had to report to boarding school and live on campus for my senior year of high school. I never quit the job. I just stopped going. I kept my uniform vest. It came in handy for my brother's wedding when I trolled my mom that the tux place gave me the wrong outfit.

The asterisk above is for horror movies. I never watched horror movies until I met my wife. Now I'm obsessed with both (note: I added that line so I'd probably get some extra special sexy time). Seriously. I hadn't seen *Friday or Halloween* or *Texas Chainsaw*. As a kid, at the various mom-and-pop video rental stores I would frequent, I would love to look at the covers of the horror movies. They terrified me and intrigued me equally. My family was not into them at all so we never rented them. I think I might have been 30 when I started watching these. *Saw. Hellraiser.* Now I love them. My wife and I were lucky enough to get a tour of the original Camp Crystal Lake for *Friday the 13th*. Two good friends of mine made B horror movies. I love them. I've written a few. They are so fun. For the entire month of October, and a few months leading up to October, we try to watch a scary movie EVERY night.

What types of movies are you generally attracted to?

All kinds. Depends on the season really. In the spring and summer it is blockbusters. In the fall, I get into more thinky, dramatic movies — the same kinds that come out for reward season. All October and even a few weeks before, as I said, it's horror movies all day long. During the month of December, we try to have a Christmas movie playing (even if just in the background) all the time.

Name a few performances that have blown you away.

So many … but here are a few that quickly come to mind. Christoph Waltz in *Inglorious Bastards*. Leo and Matt Damon in *The Departed*. Elliot Page in *Juno*.

What director's films will you always watch?

QT, Scorsese, Lord and Miller, Joss Weedon. Anything done by someone I know. Jon Favreau! James Gunn.

How much stock do you put in movie reviews?

Not much. Most reviewers watch too many movies and seem to come from a negative place. Also, I think WB owns Rotten Tomatoes.

What film are you most embarrassed to admit that you love?

There are a lot. They're not really embarrassing but probably unexpected by others. *Pitch Perfect. Cutting Edge. Love Actually. The Santa Clause. The Santa Clause 2. Star Wars* still gives me chills. So does *Indiana Jones. How to Train your Dragon 2* makes me cry.

Do you prefer to watch movies at home or in the theatre?

Obviously, the theatre. And I love a movie-loving crowd on opening day of a big blockbuster. Cheers, hooting and clapping. I'm all in. I hate late night movies where the audience has had a few drinks, especially when I'm with my kids. I love watching at home but I would instantly install a huge theatre if I could afford one that matches the quality of a real theatre. I'm talking marquees, posters, etc. Movie theatres are my happy place. I also love going to a dark, empty theatre first thing in the morning on a sunny day.

What aspect of film appeals to you the most: genre, dialogue, acting, cinematography or something else?

Film appeals to me because it is such a complicated medium that needs to work on so many levels before we really love it. There are so many steps along the way from a simple idea to a final film. So many chances for failure. So many chances for success. If someone's soul wasn't poured into every aspect of a film, it could be better. Films are this amazing cooperation of so many people.

And I like to go to another universe, at least for two hours, that reminds me that there is a lot about life and this universe we don't and won't ever get.

What advice would you give to an aspiring filmmaker?

Ok, now I'm going to harness my inner Peter-Fucking-Pan. Do or do not, there is no try. - Yoda. Just Do It - Nike. I don't like the term aspiring. You don't need permission to be a filmmaker. You don't need a 50-million-dollar budget to be a filmmaker. You have a phone and a computer. Film something. Don't expect an Oscar. Film something again. Stop asking for permission. Make something you want to make for what you can afford. You want to be a filmmaker? Make a film. All you have to do is tell a great story with the best execution that you're capable of. Never stop learning and trying new techniques. Do something that sounds hard to do. Get better at something every time. Read books. Watch films. Read books about films (like this one). Read books until they become repetitive and predictable and then move on to the next. Watch How-To videos on YouTube to learn the technology. Don't become obsessed with the current technology. Watch Master Classes. Listen to the ScriptNotes podcast. If you have the money, enter festivals, video contests and writing contests as long as you remember you won't become a filmmaker by winning something. Try to learn (at least) the basics of all aspects of filmmaking including production, directing, cinematography, editing, lighting, sound, music, special FX, how optics work, how your camera works, color grading, set building, rigging, costumes and more things I'm forgetting right now. If you know the basics, you will know your abilities and your limitations in each discipline and it will help you select your team. Get feedback on everything you make from people you trust and who will give you more than a pat on the back. Don't take feedback personally; your project can always be better. Analyze films. Analyze films from a different time than you know and judge them on the time they were released. Don't watch too many films ... you need real life too. Get drunk with friends. Understand the formulas like 'Save the Cat' but know there are no easy formulas. There are no fast passes in filmmaking. Everything you do in life is inspiration for a scene, a conversation or a character. Keep a journal. Write something every day. Just like Miles Morales in *Spider-Verse*, Neo in *The Matrix* and every other self-doubting hero in the history of storytelling, all you have to do is believe and take the leap of faith. Being a filmmaker is just a choice. Just fucking do it. If you're doing it for fame or money, you're wrong. ◆

Jaime Barbaro

45 YEARS OLD | FORMER INDUSTRIAL HYGIENIST*

Tell me a little about yourself ... Where do you live? What did you study in college? What do you do for a career?

My name is Jaime Barbaro and I currently reside in Coatesville, Pennsylvania, with my wife and two children. Originally I began my collegiate work in the study of classic literature. However, as fate intervened I performed a complete 360 and delved into the study of environmental health; specifically industrial hygiene where I received my Bachelor of Arts degree from West Chester University. From there I worked as a health and safety consultant while obtaining my Master of Science degree from Saint Joseph's University. My most current place of employment was as an industrial hygienist for Drexel University, which unfortunately I have recently left due to health considerations. Ironically, my disability allows for me to view more film outlets.

What movie(s) first inspired your love of film and why?

My inspiration for film occurred at a very early age and ultimately was derived from more than just the films themselves. It was absorbing the entire experience that made it truly special. Whether going to the theatre or just watching from our couch, it was a family event and that feeling of warmth and togetherness I still think of today while I watch movies. The first full-length feature film I ever saw was the 1979 *Star Trek: The Motion Picture*. I can still remember being in awe at the large screen and loud speaker volume of the theatre. I can almost still smell that theatre and taste the buttered popcorn. It was at this point, I was hooked. From there my addiction grew and while varied in genre, some of the earliest movies that shaped my opinion about film, and especially acting, include, but are definitely not limited to: *The Earthling, St. Helens, The Four Seasons, Silver Streak, Jaws, Meatballs, Urban Cowboy* and *Greystoke: The Legend of Tarzan, Lord of the Apes*. These are still movies that I hold dear and typically watch at a minimum on an annual basis. It is hard for me to put exactly into words why these movies mean so much to me, but to keep with the rest of my overall narrative these films exhibit exceptional acting, dialogue, plot and settings and did not seem to have to rely on the current Hollywood methodology of utilizing grotesquely large budgets, extreme special effects and computer-generated images to distract the audience from poor acting, dialogue and overall premise.

What types of movies are you generally attracted to?

While I do watch and enjoy many "Big-Star Hollywood Blockbusters," I am generally more attracted to made-for-TV movies. I feel like having a somewhat lower budget forces these networks and/or filmmakers to focus more on the story and dialogue rather than just incorporating special effects and big name actors to play parts that frankly are out of most of their realms. My preferred genres are science fiction and fantasy and I am very thankful for channels like SYFY and Paramount, which not only promote my preferred genre of film, but also meet my preferences for made-for-TV movies. If you ever get the chance, I would highly recommend the following SYFY originals: *Ogre*, *Wyvern* and *The Crooked Man* and older films such as *The Earthling*, *The Lottery*, *Alligator* and *St. Helens*.

Name a few performances that have blown you away.

While there are most likely more than a few theatrical performances that have "blown me away," a few in particular come to mind, as described below. I would like to preface that my reasoning for the actors selected was solely based on acting and dialogue. However, the plots and settings of these films undeniably both contributed and enhanced these performances. Christopher Lambert's role as John Clayton/Tarzan, Lord of the Apes in the 1984 – *Greystoke: The Legend of Tarzan*, *Lord of the Apes*, Ted Danson's role as Lemuel Gulliver in the 1996 television mini-series *Gulliver's Travels* and Gene Wilder's role as George Caldwell in the 1976 *Silver Streak*. I feel that each of these performances exhibited the utmost range and potential that these actors have ever done. The acting was serious, emotional and spot-on to the scripts. Two out of the three of these films were also true to their books and the acting acknowledged this. Other performances worth mentioning would be Tim Robbins as Andy Dufresne in the 1994 *Shawshank Redemption* and the entire casts of both the 1975 *Jaws* and 1983 *The Outsiders*.

What director's films will you always watch?

As important as the director is to the film, I feel that most people never have any clue to who these individuals are, because they're so focused on these "big name actors," when in reality the film is a combination of many disciplines which the director leads. Ultimately, the film is the director's vision and our experience is one in which he or she has planned precisely. With that said, I tend to enjoy directors that think outside of the box and utilize their own visions without significant compromise. Directors such as Kevin Smith and Rob Zombie who frequently use friends and family, John Hughes and Harold Ramis that push the envelope for writing just as they did while working for "National Lampoon" magazine, Woody Allen and Terry Gilliam that while making completely different genres of films spend the majority of their focus between dialogue and settings and Ridley Scott who could not be dissuaded when introducing the world to one of the first female heroines in film with Ripley in 1977's *Alien*.

How much stock do you put in movie reviews?

I tend to put very little stock in movie reviews, which frankly are nothing more than someone else's opinion about the same movie I'm going to watch. The material is too subjective in nature. Very seldom do these critics hold some sort of innate knowledge of the film or the director's vision that I could not have read or watched somewhere on my own. Plus, I enjoy doing my own film research and am extremely careful to not succumb to spoilers. My biggest pet peeve in the film industry, whether watching a trailer or reading an article, is when someone in the media claims they won't tell you anything substantial, but then go on to tell about how there is a shocking twist at the end. Well you just told me everything! Another pet-peeve of mine is remakes. Once again showing how out-of-touch Hollywood actually is and only interested in that bottom line. Or maybe it shows how out-of-touch society has become where people can no longer appreciate an older, black and white, subtitled and/or foreign film.

What film are you most embarrassed to admit that you love?

Believe it or not I had to put a lot of thought into this question. Unfortunately, my passion for so called "B movies" alone leaves me vulnerable for ridicule. However, it is more than likely the current

Hallmark Channel movies that I am most embarrassed to admit liking; specifically around the Christmas holiday. While I do not have the greatest answer why. I will suppose it is because of the time of year and the movies are brainless and easy to watch. They tend to follow a specific methodology that I find likeable and hold true to some of my aforementioned points about what I ultimately like about movies such as, made-for-TV, no name actors, lower budget, etc.

Do you prefer to watch movies at home or in the theatre?

While I must admit I enjoy the large viewing screen of a theatre, I would personally rather watch my movies from my home. This mostly has do with the increased ticket costs, my health conditions and generally that I have become far more agoraphobic in my middle-aged years and really do not like to be around people. Very seldom do I attend the theatre, but if I were to go, it would be to a Tuesday matinee. I would get there early to scout out my preferred seating requirements and continue to cough up a lot of sputum, so that nobody would ever want to sit near me, until the movie began.

What aspect of film appeals to you the most: genre, dialogue, acting, cinematography or something else?

All aspects of a film are of equal importance in conveying the writer's and/ or filmmaker's message and it is this culmination of techniques that will ensure a complete idea has been fully received by the audience. However, I find the dialogue to be the most appealing aspect of a film. Theoretically, one could have the most incredible premise, but without the proper dialogue spoken to connect all of the ideas the outcome loses its effect. Unfortunately, I feel that most of today's filmmakers don't concentrate enough on the writing, instead they use bathroom jokes, over-explanation and dumbing down for the masses instead of staying true to the story line. Sophomoric humor and juvenile antics are great when the premise of the film allows for it and it is not forced, otherwise stick to the script!

What advice would you give to an aspiring filmmaker?

I would advise aspiring filmmakers to never hold back and be true to their original intentions. Write, produce and direct films that truly mean something to you and what you want to say. Don't worry about offending the masses as it will ultimately dictate the direction of your art and destroy its integrity. In fact, I find that a perfect exercise is to think of all of the films that have been made that would not exist in today's sensitive censorship movement. For example a television show with absolutely no racial undertones was taken off air due to a time period flag, but others that negatively depict women, minorities and others are still allowed to thrive. If people do not like a film's premise or overall message, do not watch it, but do not allow someone else's art to be censored. ◆

Editor's Note:
Jaime Barbaro passed away on January 1, 2024, after a long battle with his health. Visiting him in the Chester County Hospital on Christmas Day, we talked about — you guessed it: movies we'd seen lately and which classics we were sharing with our kids. There isn't an 80s or 90s movie or TV show I watch today that doesn't bring back a memory of Jaime. He will be missed beyond measure.

Marc Hoffman

38 YEARS OLD | AEROSPACE ENGINEER

Tell me a little about yourself ... Where do you live? What did you study in college? What do you do for a career?

I am an aerospace engineer at Johns Hopkins Applied Physics Laboratory in Laurel, Maryland, midway between Baltimore and Washington, D.C. I received my undergraduate degree in aerospace engineering from the Pennsylvania State University and am currently finishing my masters in space systems engineering at Johns Hopkins.

One of the great things about film is that it offers an immersive medium through which amazing stories can be told, and movies played no small part in shaping my career path. I was 14 years old, already a die-hard *Star Wars* fan and had grown up watching the occasional space shuttle launch with my classmates, but had never heard of the real-life events that were depicted in *Apollo 13*. That film brought me into that historic mission as much as anything ever really could, and I was captivated. A few years later, around the time I was applying to colleges to study engineering, *October Sky* came to theatres, and I was simply hooked with studying rocket science. I later had the opportunity to meet Homer Hickam early in my career, portrayed by Jake Gyllenhaal in the film adaptation of his autobiography, "Rocket Boys," and got the chance to thank him in person for his story, which I may have never heard of if not for film.

What movie(s) first inspired your love of film and why?

It's hard to pick a particular movie that flipped the switch for my love of film because it feels like it happened at such an early age. My father was a repair technician at a cable company when my sister and I were growing up in Akron, Ohio, and one of the obvious perks was having the full channel lineup at my disposal for the entirety of my childhood. I was four-years-old when, according to my parents, I yelled, "Let's see if you bastards can do 90!" to the rest of my afternoon preschool class. I spent plenty of time outdoors, mind you, but name me anything that was playing on HBO in the 80s and 90s and I probably saw it half a dozen times. Still, movies like *Back to the Future*, *Batman* and *Star Wars* were on a different level for me. As I got older, I started to become more interested in seeing different types of movies and enjoyed *Scream*, *Romeo & Juliet* and *Toy Story* as much as I enjoyed *Independence Day*. I worked at the local theatre my senior year of high school, which was probably the most fun I've ever had while getting paid. It was around that time that *The Blair Witch Project* became a cult hit, introducing me to the world of smaller, independent films that I would come to appreciate more.

What types of movies are you generally attracted to?

I tend to gravitate toward movies that tell gripping stories; something that I ultimately lose myself in when I'm watching. You don't always know what they are, but when the truly good ones come along, you don't even realize that two and a half hours have passed as you've been hopping around Cillian Murphy's dreams with Leonardo DiCaprio and Elliot Page. Psychological thrillers, historical dramas and epic science fiction usually get it done.

Name a few performances that have blown you away.

Heath Ledger's performance in *The Dark Knight*. He literally commanded your attention in every scene he was in, and would still manage some subtle gesture or look that would pull the rug out from under you. Denzel Washington's performances in *Glory* and *Training Day*, Scarlett Johansson and Bill Murray in *Lost in Translation* and Natalie Portman in *Black Swan* are also some of my favorites.

What director's films will you always watch?

Christopher Nolan, Quentin Tarantino and still probably M. Night Shyamalan, who gave me the gift of *Unbreakable* and who I really, desperately wanted to crush it with *Glass*. Nolan had me at *Memento* and continues to deliver solid dramas that can also make you think. I love Tarantino's films as someone who has only ever taken one introductory college-level film class. He can hold a scene with heavy dialogue and do so much with it.

How much stock do you put in movie reviews?

More than I used to, and only because it's so much harder to get to the theatre to see the ones I really want to see now that I have kids. The ones I can't miss I will make time for, but reviews otherwise help me decide if I'm waiting for others until they release on video.

What film are you most embarrassed to admit that you love?

Hackers ... what can I say? I can't defend it; all I can do is love it. I have no shame in proclaiming my continued affection for *D2: The Mighty Ducks*. My wife and I also watch *Love, Actually* every year on Christmas Eve.

Do you prefer to watch movies at home or in the theatre?

I prefer the theatre, especially now that you can reserve your seats ahead of time without having to deal with the lines. It is also great to go to a theatre on opening night or to see a double feature at a drive-in, because it becomes more than just a movie, it's an experience.

What aspect of film appeals to you the most: genre, dialogue, acting, cinematography or something else?

I appreciate the truly great work that cinematographers do and will actually find myself saying out loud, "What a terrific shot!" in a crowded theatre. I will notice the long tracking shots in *Before Sunset* and am blown away by scenes like the rain sequence in *Road to Perdition*. I also like when they find unique places to put a camera for a shot, including first person perspective shots, under the wing or in the cockpit of a starship, or in the pencil sharpener on Truman Burbank's desk. I also tend to notice a film's score, which can be traced back to my affinity to listening to movie soundtracks while studying in my dorm room. To this day, I probably own more movie scores than I do music albums and have the largest number of tracks on those Spotify playlists dedicated to film music. For the record, James Newton Howard is a masterclass and is vastly underappreciated. Ultimately, whether it's through camerawork, editing, character development or narrative structure, any film that can tell a compelling story in a unique way without trying too hard will win me over.

What advice would you give to an aspiring filmmaker?

Whether its purpose is to entertain, to inspire or to express ideas, the heart of a truly good film is in its ability to tell a compelling story. Tell us yours.

◆

Stefanie Claypoole

45 YEARS OLD | MARKETING

Tell me a little about yourself ... Where do you live? What did you study in college? What do you do for a career?

I grew up about 15 miles outside of Philadelphia and now live with my husband and son in West Chester, Pensylvania. I started my college "career" at The University of Delaware where I spent three years completely squandering my opportunity (and family finances) on partying. I had an epiphany at the age of 21 to get serious about my degree (English), and was fortunate to take a few film classes at UD before I transferred to Temple University. I still wish I had at least minored in film at either of those institutions, but my English degree has actually served me pretty well. After working for a number of years as a newspaper and magazine writer, I transferred my skillset to marketing, where I am still able to write a lot, but also get to delve into web, social media, advertising and PR. I have been working at a nonprofit boys boarding school for six years and it is truly a dream job for me. Anyone who knows me would say I'm a "do-gooder," and this job makes me feel like I am doing good every day.

What movie(s) first inspired your love of film and why?

My parents divorced when I was seven, and perhaps the only thing they had in common was their love of film. That was a benefit to me and my two older brothers (but me in particular, since I was the youngest and not yet at an age where my parents were uncool), because they brought me along to every movie outing they went on, whether it was age-appropriate or not. My mom's interests leaned toward more "high brow" fare, so my earliest memories are of crowding into a packed Ritz Theater in Old City Philadelphia with her to see Kurosawa's *Ran* at the age of 10, or a tiny theatre at Temple University with 20 chairs to watch *Sugar Cane Alley* at the age of 8 or any number of Woody Allen's films (until she banned him from our viewing list). I am so appreciative of this experience; it is not something that many American children get — to be exposed to international films and worldviews at such a young age. My father, who was a filmmaker with NFL Films for 40 years, has less discriminate taste but a voracious appetite for film. My three favorite memories with him are seeing *Commando* (a movie that really jumpstarted the trend of infusing action films with comedy), watching all three Godfather films in one sitting at his insistence and, when I was in my early 20s, going to see *Boogie Nights* with him. The latter experience is one I am kind of horrified by as it is an awkward movie to watch with your dad, but the bigger memory of viewing this film is when he looked at me with awe three minutes into the film and said, "Did you see that Steffi? That was one take. No cuts!" He really taught me an appreciation for the craft. My mom taught me a love of the story.

As a tween and teen, I spent almost every afternoon at my best friend Jaime's house (also profiled in this fan section) watching movies. He had eclectic taste and an AMAZING selection of VHS, most of which he recorded from TV (remember those days?). We watched *Fast Times at Ridgemont High* almost daily (mostly because my mom said I couldn't), *Three O'Clock High*, horror movies, the skater/surfer 80s flicks like *North Shore* and *Gleaming the Cube* and all the classic 80s comedies: *Summer School, Better off Dead, Teen Wolf, Real Genius … Up the Creek* (Tim Matheson was a true comedic gem).

What types of movies are you generally attracted to?

I like every genre of film, except I've really never gotten into Westerns. But if I had to choose, I'd say comedy, even if it's a drama or action film with a healthy dose of comedy woven into it like the aforementioned *Commando* or *True Lies*. Because of my mother, I really like foreign films too, especially if I'm watching at home. As my husband can attest, home screenings usually don't work out well for me as I'm usually asleep on the couch in five minutes. However subtitles keep me alert and engaged. The last international film that really blew me away was the French film *Tell No One* in 2006, based on the Harlen Coben book. I generally have a really hard time with film adaptations of books. I haven't found a single one that has lived up to my experience of reading the story. *Mystic River, Beloved, The Color Purple …* while all great films, are not nearly on the same level as the books that inspired them. Thus, I try to avoid adaptations (except the movie *Adaptation*, which is fantastic).

Name a few performances that have blown you away.

Since I'm also the editor of this book, I feel like the men have already received sufficient love, so I'm going to focus on some performances by women. One of my earliest favorites was Debra Winger in *Terms of Endearment* — she was just so real in that role. Susan Sarandon in *Bull Durham* was just the perfect embodiment of what women want to be, and what men just want. Patricia Arquette in *True Romance*. She is so underrated but she played the character with the most appealing mix of sweet and goofy. Two other women I will always watch are Holly Hunter and Sigourney Weaver. Hunter's performances in *Raising Arizona*, *Broadcast News*, *The Firm*, *Home for the Holidays*, *Thirteen* and even the lesser known *Miss Firecracker* — she has charisma like no other. And Sigourney Weaver. Wow, such an incredible range: *The Year of Living Dangerously*, *Copycat*, *Aliens*, *Working Girl*, *Dave*, *The Ice Storm*, *Ghostbusters* … such different roles and she made them all incredibly memorable. Finally, I have to give props to Jaime Lee Curtis. *A Fish Called Wanda* is one of my favorite films of all time, and that is largely due to her performance. She also killed it in *Trading Places* and *True Lies*. She is a great comedian.

What director's films will you always watch?

Anything by the Scotts (Ridley and Tony), Spielberg, Tarantino, Coen Brothers, Scorsese, Nolan, Fincher, Lynch, PT and Wes Anderson, Guillermo Del Toro, Oliver Stone (where've you been?), Jonathan Demme, Ang Lee, Soderbergh, Alfonso Cuaron, Michael Mann, Spike Lee, Sam Mendes and Spike Jonze. I wish I had more women to list, but the ones that come to mind are Lisa Cholodenko, Sarah Polley and Nicole Holofcener.

How much stock do you put in movie reviews?

Probably more than most people because I find that I usually tend to agree with (most of) them. That said, I really only worry about reviews if I'm going to the theatre, because there is more of an expense incurred (tickets, food, babysitter) and I don't want to waste my money if I don't have to. The last time I felt like I truly wasted my money was *Glass*. Man that movie disappointed me on so many levels and I know my husband and I went into it with obscene expectations because we both loved *Unbreakable* and *Split*. That's a case where I ignored the reviews because they tend to badmouth Shyamalan, and really regretted it.

What film are you most embarrassed to admit that you love?

Films by Michael Bay and Nancy Meyers. Sometimes you just want to see things blow up; sometimes you need a good cry.

Do you prefer to watch movies at home or in the theatre?

The theatre 100%. As mentioned before, I suck at watching movies at home. I fall asleep almost instantly. I thought I would hate the rise of dine-in movie theatres, because I'm a bit of a purist and was worried the food and drinking would detract from the experience, but so far, I think it's been a great enhancement. In addition to enjoying having a cocktail or elevated snack once in a while, I LOVE reclining seating. I won't ever be able to sit in the old-style theatre seats again. I also love the camaraderie of watching a movie with other people. Hearing other people laugh always makes me laugh more than I normally would.

What aspect of film appeals to you the most: genre, dialogue, acting, cinematography or something else?

"Do you have balloons in those funny shapes? Not unless round is funny?" "I picked the wrong day to stop sniffing glue!" "If I know Mary, and I think I do, she'll invite us right in for tea and strumpets." I like all aspects of film, but the most appealing to me is dialogue (probably makes sense that I'm a writer). If I quote a funny movie and you respond in kind, we are best friends for life.

What advice would you give to an aspiring filmmaker?

I think it's the same for any art form: have passion. As a writer, I find that if my subject is dull (to me), then my output is lackluster. If you are creating something for the wrong reasons, I think that generally shows, even if you have the best people working with you. Also, every piece of the film puzzle plays an integral role. Give each of them as much attention as you can. I also strongly concur with John Ranere and Marc Hoffman's focus on the soundtrack/score. ◆

John Ranere

28 YEARS OLD | ACCOUNT MANAGER

Tell me a little about yourself ... Where do you live? What did you study in college? What do you do for a career?

I live in New Jersey. I currently work remotely from home while handling a sales territory in California. I have worked in sales for the past six years in the industrial sales industry. This career is not something I would have ever guessed I would be doing but it ended up being something I am really good at so I have stuck with it. I went to La Salle University in Philadelphia and have a BS in marketing. While in college I took many different film classes such as philosophy of film and film history 101–401.

What movie(s) first inspired your love of film and why?

Ever since I was a child I was obsessed with animation, particularly Disney/Pixar. I obviously was attracted to the colors and sounds but as I got older I became more obsessed with how they were made back in the 30s–60s with such little technology that we have today. There isn't a Disney movie that I haven't seen from Walt Disney's first full-length *Snow White and the Seven Dwarfs* (1938) to some of his live-action films such as *20,000 Leagues Under the Sea* (1954). I grew up in a house/family where watching a movie was the ending to every day. If it wasn't for my family, then I wouldn't have seen the wide range of movies that I have grown to love from *Jaws*, *Rocky* and *Indiana Jones* to *The Godfather*. It meant a lot to my dad for me to experience all of the classic movies that he also loved so this is where my love of film started.

What types of movies are you generally attracted to?

I have always been attracted to any movie that is "Based on a True Story;" I am not sure why but as soon as I see those words I instantly want to watch the movie whether I was already interested in the event or not. Some of my favorites include *The Wolf of Wall Street*, *Catch Me if You Can*, *Goodfellas*, *Into the Wild* and *The Big Short*.

Name a few performances that have blown you away.

The performances that come to my mind every time I am asked this question are Christian Bale in *The Fighter*, Heath Ledger in *The Dark Knight* and Daniel Day-Lewis in *There Will Be Blood*. The Method Acting style has always been something that blows me away. The amount of dedication and hell any method actor puts their bodies and lives through just for one performance is something that needs to be recognized and which usually always pays off.

What director's films will you always watch?

To name a few of my favorites I will always watch Quentin Tarantino, Steven Spielberg, Martin Scorsese, Francis Ford Coppola and Wes Anderson. No matter what the movie is I always know I will enjoy it if any of these directors are involved.

How much stock do you put in movie reviews?

For the most part my only form of movie reviews is Rotten Tomatoes. My rule of thumb usually is that if anything is over 60% I would want to see it, however there have been many times where a movie has been rated "rotten" and I still enjoyed the movie. I try not to pay attention or look at the ratings before I see a movie because it will ruin it for me, but with today's access to all information it is hard to avoid the negative "buzz" around a movie after it comes out.

What film are you most embarrassed to admit that you love?

The two movies that I would say I should be embarrassed about loving but I do not care because they deserve the love are *Father of the Bride* and *Father of the Bride 2*. I think both of these movies are the perfect amount of comedy mixed with Chick Flick. The Steve Martin and Martin Short chemistry is something that I cannot get enough of and will watch every time it is on TV.

Do you prefer to watch movies at home or in the theatre?

Watching movies in the theatre is 100x better than at home mainly because it is the only way to have 100% concentration on the film. Normally when

I watch a movie at home or want to get someone else to experience a movie at home that I have already seen it becomes challenging because there are too many distractions. I grew up in a family where every weekend we would go as a family to the movies to see whatever was new no matter what was out at the time. This has become something nostalgic for me so it is something I have always enjoyed and will continue the tradition.

What aspect of film appeals to you the most: genre, dialogue, acting, cinematography or something else?

Dialogue and acting is probably what appeals to me the most. When something is written badly or has bad acting no matter how good the cinematography is, the movie will automatically be bad. It is always nearly impossible to ignore when a movie has bad acting and horrible dialogue and it takes away from everything else that went into making the film.

What advice would you give to an aspiring filmmaker?

I am not a filmmaker so I am not really in the position to give film advice, however I would say to make sure they have good dialogue, spend time on casting to make sure it is the best fit and always make sure the film has a good soundtrack. ◆

Joshua Dwyer

40 YEARS OLD | ENGLISH TEACHER

Tell me a little about yourself ... Where do you live? What did you study in college? What do you do for a career?

I grew up outside Philadelphia in a suburb named Havertown. The town itself was comprised of mostly white Irish/Italian Catholic people that did not value culture. Most of the interests were based off of or on sports. People obviously went to the movies, but I do not remember anyone ever talking about the components of film. It wasn't until taking a few film classes in one of the three colleges that I attended that I grasped how a film could be studied, broken down and analyzed. I fell in love with the terminology and how people could see themes or ideas that were not present to me before examining a film. I am currently a high school English teacher and use movies to help students understand literature on a deeper level. Because most are more passionate about movies, it is easy to display how to analyze art with this medium.

What movie(s) first inspired your love of film and why?

Growing up in the 80s, I always enjoyed comedies and action films, but wasn't exposed to many dramas or Oscar-winning movies. I knew there were awards and had seen some of the more serious pieces, but they did not have an impact on me. I know this is cliché, especially for my generation, but it wasn't until I saw *Pulp Fiction* in the theatre that I fell in love with film. I remember one of my teachers told me about this new director and how great he was, and that I needed to see this movie. I walked out of the theatre with so many emotions. I was amazed by the acting, screenplay, cinematography and obviously the non-chronological order of the film. Similar to many others' reactions, after that I needed to see everything this guy Tarantino had created or been influenced by. I then found the film *True Romance* and it instantly became my favorite film. It is one movie that I still put on once or twice a year and appreciate its beauty.

What types of movies are you generally attracted to?

I am huge fan of realism. Films that do not use many special effects to draw the viewer in and move him/her. Independent films usually fall under this category and have strong and/or complex plotlines and characters. The same can be said for the literature I read. I am not drawn toward fantasy or sci-fi films, but I will still watch or read pieces, and give them a chance. Films such as *Garden State* (which I wrote a major paper on in college) that are simple but display a solid character arc and development help people better understand the human condition. *Adaptation* could be another example of this type of idea. Here, the art is stripped down and you can enjoy the ideas in a more clear sense.

Name a few performances that have blown you away.

I have named *True Romance* as my favorite film, because there are some amazing performances in this film. Watching Walken and Hopper in the interrogation scene is like watching two acting heavyweights duke it out on the screen. I can watch that scene over and over again! There are a few other scenes in this film such as Gary Oldman as Drexel, but others should not be overlooked. Gandolfini's introduction to the public was a great first performance, and many others in this film. If I had to narrow it down to a few performances that have blown me away, they would be: James Dean *Rebel Without a Cause*, Marlon Brando *A Streetcar Named Desire*, Meryl Streep in anything, Sissy Spacek *Coal Miner's Daughter* (my mom's favorite), Phillip Seymour Hoffman *Capote*, Mickey Rourke *The Wrestler* and Forrest Whitaker *The Color of Money* (short scene, but he steals the show in this movie).

What director's films will you always watch?

Sadly, it wasn't until much later in my life that I started to utilize the auteur theory where you understand that the director is the driving creative force behind a film. Too many times I would see an actor's excellent performance and view another future film that they starred in and usually, was let down. For a few years, I wasted money at the box office expecting to see another great film merely because one of my favorite actors was in that piece. Similar to many people of my generation, I grew up watching

Tarantino films, and although the last few movies he has created I question, this director will always have a place in my heart. I enjoy watching Oliver Stone movies over and over again, because I think they become better with each viewing. I also think that Christopher Nolan is underrated when talking about all of the great directors. The Coen brothers have produced films that I think are timeless and have a sense of humor that is on another level. And last, but not least Scorsese. The only issue I have with his films is that he has a system that he sticks to, and it is quite obvious after a while. For instance, he usually uses the Rolling Stones in his soundtracks.

How much stock do you put in movie reviews?

I tell my students that Wikipedia is not a bad place to start when researching a subject, but to not put a bunch of stock in what is written on that site. The same could be said about movie reviews. I start with a review then look at other things pertaining to the film. Whether it is the director, subject matter or actors, I consider a bunch of things before spending money to see a movie in the theatre.

What film are you most embarrassed to admit that you love?

Most of my guilty pleasure films come from the 80s. Movies such as *Can't Buy Me Love* or *Weird Science* that are funny, but do not have much depth. After reading an article in the New Yorker about John Hughes pertaining to the #MeToo movement, I am embarrassed to watch his films now because they did not age well.

Do you prefer to watch movies at home or in the theatre?

No question, I prefer to watch movies in a theatre. The smell of freshly popped popcorn alone makes the experience better. Also, I feel that there is an energy when seeing a movie in a full theatre that you cannot get out of watching it at home with a few people. Comedies are funnier and thrillers have more impact when a larger group of people have the same reactions.

What aspect of film appeals to you the most: genre, dialogue, acting, cinematography or something else?

I am a huge fan of the spoken word, so dialogue would have to be what appeals the most to me. As an English teacher, we quote important lines from literature and film is no different. They are two different mediums, but the words always stick out when people refer to each one. I also enjoy cinematography too because I like to see the choices the cinematographer/director made in order to move the viewer in a certain way.

What advice would you give to an aspiring filmmaker?

I do not know because this craft is so intense. I would not even know where to start other than they must have passion that overrides the ideas, opinions and thoughts of others. ◆

P. Edward Claypoole

41 YEARS OLD
PROCUREMENT-FULL TIME/DIRECTOR-CREATOR PART TIME

What movie(s) first inspired your love of film and why?

I talk about this in-depth in the introduction to this book, but I am an 80s kid, so *E.T.*, *Goonies*, *The Neverending Story*, *The Last Starfighter*, *Condorman*, *Back To The Future*, *Ferris Bueller's Day Off*, *The Karate Kid*, *Raiders of the Lost Ark*, *Top Gun*, *Ghostbusters* and *Home Alone* which was actually 1990 ... pretty much every movie I saw as a child, I was absolutely amazed by them all. As I got into my teens it changed to more grownup themes and I got to see some real classics ... *Beverly Hills Cop*, *Die Hard*, *Lethal Weapon*, *Seven*, *Pulp Fiction*, *The Silence of The Lambs*, *Fight Club* and *Scream*.

What types of movies are you generally attracted to?

I like all genres of film and find them all entertaining, however my first choice would be the thriller — movies that keep me guessing the whole movie and have a great plot twist, such as *The Game*, *Seven*, *The Sixth Sense* and *The Usual Suspects*. If you can give me a great scare, I'm down for a scary movie anytime, but mostly around Halloween and one of my favorites is *Scream*. I am also a big fan of comedies. *Raising Arizona*, *Coming to America*, *Napoleon Dynamite*, *There's Something About Mary*, *Juno*, *The Hangover*, *The Big Lebowski* and *Sideways* are some favorites. Documentaries are also a big part of my life. I was attracted to documentary filmmaking while in school and since then have completed two documentaries in the last three years. I watch them whenever I can to learn new stories, but also to learn about the craft. *Blackfish*, *Super Size Me*, *The Cove*, *An Inconvenient Truth* and *Won't You Be My Neighbor* have all been special to me.

Name a few performances that have blown you away.

Leonardo DiCaprio in *The Revenant*. Steve Martin in *Father of The Bride*. Morgan Freeman and Tim Robbins in *The Shawshank Redemption*. Dustin

Hoffman in *Rain Man*. Frances McDormand in *Fargo*. Tom Cruise in *Jerry Maguire*. Tom Hanks in *Forrest Gump* and *Philadelphia*. Philip Seymour Hoffman, Burt Reynolds and Mark Wahlberg in *Boogie Nights*. Paul Giamatti in *Sideways*. Jack Nicholson in *The Shining*. Charlize Theron in *Monster*. Russell Crowe in *The Insider*.

What director's films will you always watch?

Quentin Tarantino, Steven Spielberg, Wes Anderson, Tony Scott, M. Night Shyamalan, David Fincher, Christopher Nolan, Martin Scorsese and Clint Eastwood.

How much stock do you put in movie reviews?

Absolutely nothing. Some movies that had bad reviews I actually loved, and vice versa. If you and I sat down and reviewed a movie, my review and your review would be completely different, even if our review was positive and we recommended people seeing it. I very rarely will read reviews and if I do, they never persuade me to see or not to see a movie. The best most recent example I can give is the movie *Serenity* starring Matthew McConaughey and Anne Hathaway. I saw the trailer in the movie theatre for this movie and I thought it looked awesome. Well, the movies' release was delayed several times, which is never a good sign, and the reviews online were just horrible. I was constantly reading them because I was checking to see when it was going to finally be released. When it was released it went right to on demand and I rented it the same night … and it was indeed horrible. Moral of this story is that I had made up my mind when I first saw that trailer, there was not a review out there that was going to persuade me to change my mind.

What film are you most embarrassed to admit that you love?

I'm not sure I will ever admit that I'm actually embarrassed to like a certain film, there may be laughs among friends when discussing it, but if I like a movie, I like it, that's it. Some of the films that gained laughs from friends when discussing them are *The Cutting Edge*, *Fool's Gold* and *Father of the Bride*.

Do you prefer to watch movies at home or in the theatre?

The theatre is the place to be; the atmosphere is everything. Feeding off of others' laughter, sadness or surprise makes the whole experience better. It's definitely nice that TV's have gotten bigger, thinner and less expensive, so my setup at home is pretty nice, too.

What aspect of film appeals to you the most: genre, dialogue, acting, cinematography or something else?

I think they all have their own special part to making a movie complete. If I were to pick one over the other I would go with cinematography. Cinematography to me is the art piece of the film. Being able to frame a scene perfectly takes great patience and lots of experience. Ever watch a film and out of nowhere you think, or turn to the person next to you and say, "great shot!" … that's what I enjoy. It's the equivalent of walking into a museum and looking at an oil masterpiece or a fine-art photograph and thinking, "what a beautiful shot."

What advice would you give to an aspiring filmmaker?

Just go out and do it. I think most of us think of great ideas but don't act on them. We get caught up in the cost, or convince ourselves no one will watch or care about it, and in all honesty who cares. I love film because I love stories and I love telling stories. If I was worried every time I made a film if someone was going to watch it, I wouldn't make anything. If you put your heart into something and really give it your all, it will find its audience. ◆

Alex Ryan

27 YEARS OLD | MEDIA MANAGER

Tell me a little about yourself ... Where do you live? What did you study in college? What do you do for a career?

I currently live in Philadelphia. I went to college at the University of Pittsburgh where I studied communications and digital media. I work at a marketing agency that specializes in digital media and customer experience. I am a media manager, which means that I develop strategy for, build, manage and report on a variety of digital media campaigns on platforms such as Facebook, The Trade Desk, Instagram, LinkedIn and Google.

What movie(s) first inspired your love of film and why?

My dad was (and still is) a big movie buff, and always shared this with me. Growing up with a dad who was older, I have gotten exposure to different types of movies than a lot of my other friends. In addition to watching popular movies from the decade/year, my dad always made it a point to introduce me to "the classics." This ranged from old westerns to original horror movies like *Dracula* to the great mob movies like the *Godfather* trilogy and *Scarface*. I remember several times where I would mention a movie that was coming out and he would make us watch the original before seeing the new version.

What types of movies are you generally attracted to?

I really love historical fiction. I like movies that are historically accurate where I can learn a bit about a period in time while also being entertained by a story. *Gladiator*, *Saving Private Ryan*, *Darkest Hour*, *Braveheart*, *Milk*, *Titanic*. There are certain actors/actresses that if they are in a movie, regardless of what it is about, I'll watch it. They just give it a certain validity without me even knowing anything about the movie. A few of those for me are Leonardo DiCaprio, Brad Pitt, Joseph Gordon-Levitt, Tom Hanks, Joaquin Phoenix, Eddie Redmayne and Meryl Streep (I swear I don't hate women, but I'm just now realizing that in this particular case, there are a lot more men on this list of "I'll see any movie if this person is in it.").

Name a few performances that have blown you away.

Heath Ledger, *The Dark Knight*
Rami Malek, *Bohemian Rhapsody*
Eddie Redmayne, *The Danish Girl*
Natalie Portman, *Black Swan*
Leonardo DiCaprio, *The Wolf of Wall Street*

What director's films will you always watch?

I don't really have a favorite director, but I always enjoy Wes Anderson's films. *The Grand Budapest Hotel* is one of my favorite movies of all time. I love all of the little details throughout the movie, I love the cuts (think: the scene where he's calling for help and all of the different hotel managers have to stop what they're doing to answer and then pass it along to the next). I love the overall whimsical feeling behind all of it.

How much stock do you put in movie reviews?

Not a ton. I always look at Rotten Tomatoes, but I pretty much lost all faith in reviews when *Manchester by the Sea* won a bunch of awards and got a 96% on Rotten Tomatoes, because that was one of the worst films I have ever seen.

What film are you most embarrassed to admit that you love?

I'm embarrassed to admit HOW much I love *Pirates of the Caribbean* (let's remember that I saw it seven times in theatres and then was Jack Sparrow three years in a row for Halloween).

Do you prefer to watch movies at home or in the theatre?

In the theatre, but I don't get there anywhere near enough. I would think that the movies that would spring to mind would be dramas, made memorable by being able to see them on the big screen, but the ones that I'm thinking about are all comedies. I vividly remember seeing *Anchorman* and *Wedding Crashers* in theatres and laughing so hard that I couldn't breathe. Those are the movies that I remember coming out of the theatre and wanting to tell everyone that I could how funny the movie was. I don't particularly remember seeing any amazing dramas in theatres, or none that are sticking out more-so than others. I think that's because I typically see a bunch of movies that win awards after Oscar season, so by then all of the "best movies" of the year are already out of theatres. I guess that's the mark for me of seeing a great movie in theatres — wanting to get out and immediately talk about it with someone else, therefore creating a shared experience.

What aspect of film appeals to you the most: genre, dialogue, acting, cinematography or something else?

Dialogue is definitely big. If it doesn't flow in a realistic way or feels forced, I'll lose interest. Also if there's too much of a buildup (20–30 minutes) with no real storyline development, I'll lose interest. The story has to have forward momentum.

What advice would you give to an aspiring filmmaker?

Keep the integrity of the story in mind. Make it accurate and genuine. ◆

Taylor McGrory

27 YEARS OLD | ACCOUNT EXECUTIVE

Tell me a little about yourself ... Where do you live? What did you study in college? What do you do for a career?

I currently live in Philadelphia, Pennsylvania, but I was born and raised in New Jersey. I attended Rutgers University, where I studied marketing, earning my B.A. in 2014. I've been working as an Account Executive at a fleet management company called ARI for about two years.

What movie(s) first inspired your love of film and why?

Forrest Gump. I don't know why, but I loved the film as a child and would watch it on repeat at an inappropriate age. I think I was attracted to the scenes depicting the war in Vietnam.

What types of movies are you generally attracted to?

Crime. I've always been drawn to the seedy underbelly of what seems to be an otherwise mundane existence. *The Usual Suspects*, *The Town*, *Donnie Brasco* and *Blow* to name a few. War. Growing up I wanted to be a marine and I think that's carried over into my adult life, drawing me toward these types of films. *Saving Private Ryan*, *Black Hawk Down*, *Hacksaw Ridge* and *Full Metal Jacket*. I also enjoy historical epics such as *Lincoln*, *Bridge of Spies* and *Schindler's List*.

Name a few performances that have blown you away

Anthony Hopkins as Hannibal Lecter in *Silence of the Lambs*. His ability to portray subtle changes of emotion with only his eyes. Rarely blinking and capturing you with his gaze. It was almost reptilian. Daniel Day-Lewis as Bill "The Butcher" in *Gangs of New York*. It's more about his dedication to his craft than performance itself. He's renowned for his method acting and his preparation for this film was no different. He apparently had his own eyeball covered in a prosthetic glass so he could tap the tip of a knife to his eye without blinking.

What director's films will you always watch?

Tarantino – *Once Upon a Time in Hollywood, Inglorious Basterds*
Spielberg – *Jurassic Park, Jaws, Catch Me If You Can*
Scorsese – *Casino, Goodfellas, The Departed*
Wes Anderson – *The Grand Budapest Hotel*

How much stock do you put in movie reviews?

Little to none.

What film are you most embarrassed to admit that you love?

500 Days of Summer and *A.I – Artificial Intelligence* – both make me cry
every time.

Do you prefer to watch movies at home or in the theatre?

There's something nostalgic about going to the movies for me. I remember
my father taking me to go see matinees during the sweltering dog days of
summer. We would escape the heat, get a big bucket of buttery popcorn and
our favorite candy (Raisinets). The memories come flooding back every
time I go to the theatre, it's something I can't recreate at home.

What aspect of film appeals to you the most: genre, dialogue, acting, cinematography or something else?

The acting and cinematography are the two main criteria that make a good
film. In my opinion, anyway.

What advice would you give to an aspiring filmmaker?

Find an obscure comic, bring it back to relevancy and make an entire series
of films. ◆

Clinton Shippen

40 YEARS OLD | IT

Tell me a little about yourself ... Where do you live? What did you study in college? What do you do for a career?

I live in Collegeville, Pennsylvania. I studied business management/creative writing in college. I work in IT by day and write for film/TV in my free time.

What movie(s) first inspired your love of film and why?

Raiders of the Lost Ark is the first movie I remember that I actually wanted to be the main character; traveling the world to cool dark mysterious places and fighting bad guys along the way. There was something magical about *Indiana Jones* when I was at that age.

What types of movies are you generally attracted to?

All films, but usually science fiction or thrillers.

Name a few performances that have blown you away.

Anthony Hopkins in *Silence of the Lambs* is one of my favorite characters of all time. Denzel Washington in *Cry Freedom*. Robin Williams in *Good Will Hunting*. Morgan Freeman in *The Shawshank Redemption*.

What director's films will you always watch?

Tarantino, Spike Lee and James Cameron.

How much stock do you put in movie reviews?

Very little; I respect others' opinions but films are something I need to see myself to judge.

What film are you most embarrassed to admit that you love?

I wouldn't say I'm embarrassed but I have a soft spot for teen comedies from the 80s, e.g., *Weird Science*, *Better Off Dead*, *Ferris Buellers' Day Off*. Whenever they're on TV I can't resist watching them.

Do you prefer to watch movies at home or in the theatre?

It used to be the theatre but with having kids I'm more comfortable at home; the convenience is more abundant there with no travel time and I can pause what I'm watching for restroom breaks which occur more frequently now that I'm older.

What aspect of film appeals to you the most: genre, dialogue, acting, cinematography or something else?

I'm more into dialogue and acting ... the way it's captured doesn't move me as much as the word and actual performance.

What advice would you give to an aspiring filmmaker?

Own your vision as much as possible, this way you aren't leaving anything up to chance or anyone else. This way, you get exactly what you want and the audience sees the closest interpretation of your vision of the film. ◆

Andrew K.

40 YEARS OLD | SMALL BUSINESS OWNER

Tell me a little about yourself ... Where do you live? What did you study in college? What do you do for a career?

I was born and raised just outside Philadelphia. I currently reside in Philly. I graduated from Arizona State University with a Bachelor of Science degree majoring in Spanish. I currently run a small family-owned furniture and design business that has a retail location in New Jersey.

What movie(s) first inspired your love of film and why?

The Maltese Falcon was the first movie where I became enamored with cinematic dialogue and even though I first saw it 60 years after its original release, it still resonates with me today. I consider it the best script of all time and could watch that movie over and over again.

What types of movies are you generally attracted to?

There is not one specific genre that I am attracted to but I tend to choose movies that feature talented actors and actresses because I feel they have more choice in the movies they sign on to do and perhaps creative freedom which ultimately makes for a better picture.

Name a few performances that have blown you away.

One of the main performances that comes to mind would be the movie *Gladiator*. I feel that the creative team was able to combine successful elements of similarly plotted movies and reintroduce it in their own unique likeness. It is a great story with terrific dialogue, amazing sound and an original score which makes this one of my favorite movies of all time.

What director's films will you always watch?

There isn't a particular director that I always watch but I have probably seen all of Quentin Tarantino, Christopher Nolan and Antoine Fuqua's movies.

How much stock do you put in movie reviews?

I put zero stock into movie reviews. My feeling is that critics have their own agenda that they are always trying to push.

What film are you most embarrassed to admit that you love?

I'm not embarrassed to admit that I love any film.

Do you prefer to watch movies at home or in the theatre?

I prefer to watch movies at home unless it is a big budget action adventure film that must be seen on the big screen, such as *Jurassic Park*.

What aspect of film appeals to you the most: genre, dialogue, acting, cinematography or something else?

The aspect of film that most appeals to me is the dialogue. In my opinion, this is where the film begins and ends. The script is the driving force of the movie and you can't have a good movie without a well-written script. Even a boring or silly plot can ultimately be an entertaining movie with an innovative script and a cast that can execute the writer's vision. A recent example would be Tarantino's *The Hateful Eight*, which follows the tale of eight people in a cabin post-Civil War in Wyoming. From a plot standpoint, there is much to be desired, yet the clever dialogue provides a witty and humorous film.

What advice would you give to an aspiring filmmaker?

My advice would be to find a previously successful story or idea that has a relatable impact to the filmmaker's own life and creatively reconstruct that success. I imagine to an aspiring filmmaker it would be extremely difficult to create a completely original film from scratch, whereas using a template from someone else's success and reinventing it in their own vision might be an easier way to break into a very difficult business. ◆

Steve A.

46 YEARS OLD | OPERATIONS

Tell me a little about yourself ... Where do you live? What did you study in college? What do you do for a career?

I live in Oaks, Pennsylvania, and I'm in Operations.

What movie(s) first inspired your love of film and why?

I saw *Star Wars* in 1977 when I was three years old which laid the foundation for my love of film. A space western with alien creatures, lasers and spaceships ticked every box of my little-boy checklist.

What types of movies are you generally attracted to?

Genre films, animation, 1970s–80s Italian Horror, South Korean films and movies with great storytelling.

Name a few performances that have blown you away.

Specifically, Rinko Kikiuchi's performance in *Babel* haunts me to this day.

What director's films will you always watch?

Tarantino, Guillermo del Toro, Nolan, Miyazaki, early Dario Argento Giallos, Hitchcock, Park Chan-wook … too many to list really. I watch a lot of movies.

How much stock do you put in movie reviews?

Not much, especially nowadays. I feel that reviews are biased positively or negatively toward a social agenda and not whether a film was good or bad technically and narratively. I love Rex Reed's reviews though.

What film are you most embarrassed to admit that you love?

Krull.

Do you prefer to watch movies at home or in the theatre?

I have to watch Marvel movies in the theatre for the whole sensory experience. Otherwise, my home theatre does the job.

What aspect of film appeals to you the most: genre, dialogue, acting, cinematography or something else?

Technical prowess behind the camera always appeals to me. Complicated tracking and crane shots. Color saturation or lack thereof. A good soundtrack that matches the tone of the film. Great, well-thought out dialogue for sure. Quirky, relatable characters.

What advice would you give to an aspiring filmmaker?

Tell interesting stories, do what you love and watch tons of movies. ◆

Acknowledgements

First and foremost, I'd like to thank my wife, Stefanie, who is a writer/editor and I am not, but when I told her I wanted to do this, she told me to go for it, never doubting me.

I'd like to thank my parents, who knew at a young age that I wanted something to do with filmmaking and they never discouraged me. They told me to go after whatever made me happy. I have and I am happy.

I'd like to thank all of my teachers at The Art Institute of Philadelphia, which no longer exists. I learned a lot there, and I use a lot of that knowledge every day. I really enjoyed that learning experience.

I'd like to thank every filmmaker that I interviewed for this book. I had to convince them I was going to do this, considering I have never done this before. They believed in me and I believe in them. I love what they do, and I hope this book reflects that.

I'd like to also thank the Film Festival employees. Once again I had to convince a bunch of people that I was really writing a book. They got back to me, and said they would help, and I am indebted to them for that.

Finally, I'd like to thank the fans. Most of the fans are my friends, but you know how that works. You tell a bunch of friends you want their input on something, everything turns into a joke and nothing ever gets done. These fans were different. I told them what I was trying to do, and they supported me. I am thankful for that.

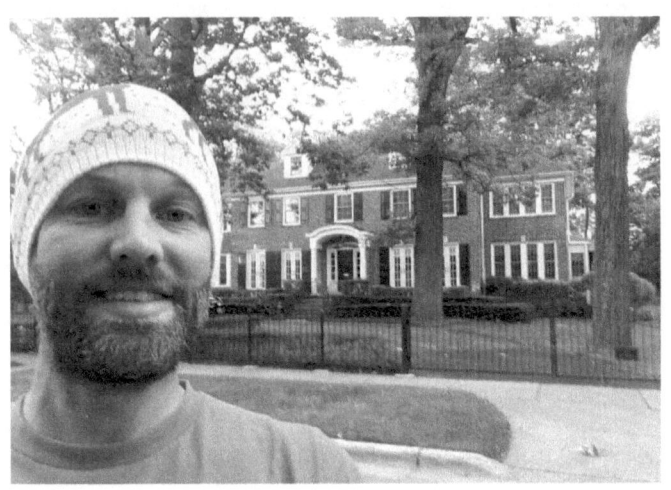

In front of the Home Alone house, Winnetka, IL.

◆

P. Edward Claypoole is a director, producer and writer residing in West Chester, PA. He graduated with a degree in Video Production from the Art Institute of Philadelphia in 2005. His first short film, *The One Percent: The Mark Himebaugh Story*, premiered at the Cape May Film Festival in 2016.